MORE BONBONS & TASTY TREATS

THAT NOURISH YOUR SPIRIT

FAITH LYNELLA

These BonBons contain no calories, but will nourish your mind and spirit. Savor and enjoy. Nibble in any order that suits you.

Warning: When consumed, the contents of this book has the power to change your life!

Radiant Library.

Radiant Library is an imprint of
Off the Page Press

Greg
Play your music
be filled with Ginkles
Faith

COPYRIGHT

More BonBons & Tasty Treats that Nourish Your Spirit
Faith Lynella (1944)
Also published as Dr. Lynella Grant and Lynella Faith Grant

You might also like *BonBons to Sweeten Your Daily Life* © 1996 (Volume 1, this being Volume 2)

http://faithlynella.com
http://offthepagepress.com

Foreword
Each BonBon is a Treat

I've been writing BonBons since 1990. Each comes to me as a love letter from my wiser nature. The first collection of them was published in 1994 as *BonBons to Sweeten Your Daily Life*. That's over 20 years ago! And I've continued to write them over the years.

Some of the BonBons in this second volume have already been published in books and articles I've written (like *Pockets of Air* and *Naked Visionary*). Or they might have been posted on one of my websites. But most of those included in this volume are being published for the first time.

Every chapter, except the first and the last, is filled with BonBons—about 75 of them. The last chapter is Chocolate Chips, short nibbles of just a tasty bite or two.

I am always humbled when putting a collection of BonBons together. It is as though I'm reading what someone else wrote. I cannot believe I would have been able to express a fragile or impossible-to-capture idea in just that way.

For in truth, my everyday self didn't write them, so they are as new and instructive for me as for any other reader. Every BonBon can stand on its own, and most of them are evergreen or timeless. Many explore the concerns we all share, and they bring us to recognize our common humanity more deeply.

Since they continue to arrive of their own accord, I'm already starting to collect volume 3. They may also be published in audio and/or video formats, so BonBons can reach a larger audience.

Getting the Message Out

A book is long, a BonBon is shorter, but a slogan brief enough to fit on a mug or T-shirt is shortest of all. But it's possible for each of them to deliver the same message—and to make you feel the same clarity inside. Does it strike a spark of insight in the reader?

Whether a concept comes in printed form within two covers, in "chocolate" form as a BonBon, or as a printed mug or T-shirt that says what's on your mind, please take these words to heart. They speak to the human experience, to the highs and lows each of us encounters. I hope they can brighten your day, lighten your load, and strengthen your relationships now and for the long haul.

I realized many more people will read a T-shirt that's worn in public than will ever read my books. Same sentiment, different format. Same binkle or energy, but easier to share. And I've designed a lot of other T-shirts or mugs based on what I've been writing over the years. For example:

I even started an online store for all my custom **T-shirts: http://seizethesparkshirts.com**

Mugs and jewelry with my quotes are found in my online store: **http://spreesy.com/seizethespark**

You might find just the one you'd like to wear or give to somebody else.

Binkles

Faith Lynella

CONTENTS

Extended Contents

Introduction

CHOCOLATES!!

For me?

Ooooh! They look so good I could eat the whole box!

Let's see now—where should I start?

Every box of chocolate BonBons comes as a treat and a choice. Which kind to eat first?

How many do I dare to have now? Do I have to share?

The answers should all be "Suit yourself—whatever you like!"

Consider this book your special box of chocolate BonBons. Open it, then consume as much as you desire, whenever you desire. Eat one; eat several. They are rich enough that you probably can't eat them all in one sitting. Some may take some chewing. As with the best candy, savor it; enjoy it; linger over it. It's all a matter of your personal taste.

For the health conscious, these are calorie-free, cholesterol free, and won't give you zits or melt in the hot car. They will, however, energize and enliven you mentally, emotionally and spiritually. Reading them helps you notice much that is special in your everyday world. Enjoy them all you want— share if you like...

The box will never be empty
and neither will your life

Chapter 1
What Is a BonBon?

Treat Yourself to Something Delicious

BonBons are calorie free, fun, uplifting, and totally satisfying for your mind and heart. Enjoy them yourself and share with a friend. Each BonBon can enrich your day, gladden your soul, and provide fresh awareness of your wondrous life.

BonBons are written by my heart and higher awareness. They arrive with a completeness and uniqueness that always seem to surprise me. It's never something I've thought out ahead of time—quite the contrary. BonBons come *to me* and *through me*, but it is always evident they don't come *from me*.

I don't write BonBons. My role is closer to transcription, as they whisper in my ear. Most of them come to me fully formed, each having its own wording and cadence built in. Each arrives with an upbeat, coherent message that forestalls being tinkered with.

I cannot simply decide to write one, for it would have a very different energy—a more rational and ordinary energy.

They arrive when they please—without warning. And they defy being reworked so it becomes something else.

A new BonBon comes with a "Howdy" the heart recognizes. During the time when a person reads one, the reader's own clear-seeing wisdom is front and center. Someone cannot get the whole message only by using everyday logic. But rather, you recognize that's a "big T Truth you know somehow." Something within yourself can speak that language. For what it communicates doesn't depend on the words alone.

BonBons speak from a larger, more expansive, and comprehending view than our everyday one. Even the BonBons that are quirky or just for fun have a grain of higher truth and a dollop of uplifting energy. Any one of them could possibly be life changing if it speaks to your heart of hearts.

My brain plays a secondary role as a BonBon comes together (with perhaps minor editing later). But my internal editor stands aside and doesn't interfere with the process. To do much more to it, or to add more arguments in order to make a point, would violate the spirit of the message. The process cannot be controlled or forced by me, much as I might try to make it happen.

A BONBON'S MESSAGE CHANGES AS YOU DO

Reading a BonBon pulls a person out of the rational way of thinking—for the moment anyway. It speaks to you at the level where your own wisdom resides. Some readers have told me they feel BonBons are like poetry. And like poetry, the words impart meaning beyond what the rational mind can grasp.

What any BonBon conveys can alter over time or with re-reading because each of us is changing and growing. And the needs in our lives don't remain the same. You could probably open this book to any page and find that particular BonBon somehow saying exactly what you need to hear. Try it.

Most of them are only a page or so, but **each BonBon has a binkle center** (later). Every one of them has a message that is more than the sum of the words on the page. For they echo deeper truths that nourish the heart and spirit, as well as the mind. Reading BonBons provides an uplifting treat for your spirit, with a brief respite from the demands and outrages of life.

I like to say "my favorite place to be is where the BonBons come." That's a sign I'm in total alignment with myself, along with an awareness beyond myself. A new one feels like getting a telegram that is not defined by my customary consciousness. But what arrives has the power to make me see more clearly and stay rooted in the moral high ground. That's why I live with a wish to be in the space where BonBons come.

THE BINKLE CENTER

A binkle is the energy created when people really connect, or when you're inspired or feel most alive.

A binkle is a *measure of energy*, the kind that uplifts and inspires. It's a zizz!—the smallest bit of upbeat energy that you can sense or share with another person.

My discovery of the binkle happened in 1992. The concept came together in a short-lived flash of great clarity and intensity. It ended with the statement, "It's called the binkle." So, its name was given to me, but I've gotten to know more about binkle power through the living of it.

Since, then I've been using binkles in the way I relate to whatever happens to me. I'm determined to experience as many binkles as I can every day, in as much variety as possible. Binkle energy keeps me positive, grateful, and charged up. It also informs how I relate to other people, spend my time, and what I write.

Every binkle brings a small pocket of peace and breathing room, along with the uplifting energy boost. Said the other way around: in every feel-good experience, it's possible to find a binkle. Binkles are a measure of the energy itself, varying from teeny to massive.

A binkle delivers a zizz of highly-charged energy. Some are mildly-pleasant ripples and others are head-to-toe zaps. Multiple binkles can build on each other in a delightful way. How or why the binkle happened is secondary to the sensation, the clarity, and the energy surge that's felt.

A view that "takes your breath away" or experiencing something genuine and abiding can be felt as "high binkle" because of the expansive and above-the-fray feelings that are so evident.

"Binkle" can be a noun or a verb. Consider it the fuel for our creative impulses—as well as the reward for having them. Its impact on a person's state of mind is immediate. You can, on occasion, feel such energetic surges without having a clue as to why. Even then t there is a feeling of "just right" about it.

The binkle is a measure of high-octane, lift-off energy— much like a watt or an ohm. But rather than its intensity level being registered by an electronic device, *you sense it with your body.* Notice that *a binkle is the energy that is experienced*—not the reason the binkle happened, or the situation in which it occurred.

Binkles are not the thoughts you have about how you feel. They are not about whether or not you like something. That binkle sensation is either present, or it isn't, when something happens. For its energetic charge cannot be faked.

WE ABSOLUTELY LOVE THAT FEELING

When we say something touches us deeply, that's a sign of binkle energy being present. Something deep within registers the sensation and is being nurtured. If you reflect back on your happiest times, you will probably recall that special sensation was present, and probably felt by all the participants.

Binkles are also there when we "walk on air" because we disengage from our ordinary frame of reference and the weight of the world.

Binkles are exactly the same energy that fuels creativity and peak experiences. They are exactly the same energy that fills your heart with joy, or wonder or, dare I say—love. Each is brief, but they can build on each other and grow in intensity. They are the energy of *feeling alive and happy* inside.

Look for them, from the leap of your heart when you sense one, to the residual afterglow that remind you "life is good." Binkles are sensed as bright spots sprinkled through a person's everyday life—each a "now moment" that's being felt energetically—by all of yourself.

If you question the need for a separate word for this special energy, ask yourself: when you have had a surge of uplifting energy or a special moment, didn't you give credit to the circumstances or the other people present? You attributed that feeling to what occurred, while failing to notice the quality of energy responsible for it.

Once you're attuned to spotting binkle energy, it is second nature to encounter them almost anywhere, or in any situation.

It is not your mind that recognizes binkles, or even your emotions, but *your whole self.* Each binkle experience provides a brief moment of *sensing yourself altogether whole*—with nothing lacking. They start our creative juices flowing and provide a reminder that what you really care about the most *is* important. Vitally important. So even though this word "binkle" may be new to you, you are already sensitized to how they "ring your bell" when you feel them.

BonBons have a special energy and vibration

About a year after the first book of BonBons was published, my son Ross read the entire book cover to cover one weekend. Ross was a college student at the time.

Although the Lunchbox Notes had been written to him, and had been avidly discussed when he received them day-in-and-day-out, many of the BonBons in it were new to him. Or they'd only been read one at a time years before.

This was the equivalent of him eating the whole box of chocolates in one sitting. Ross also has the advantage of knowing me and how I think rather intimately. Up until that cover-to-cover reading, he'd protest, "Why would I need to read a book of BonBons? They all just sound like you do all the time."

His next visit home from college, Ross told me how much he enjoyed certain ones. It was a conversation I cherished and truly enjoyed, for his insights were right on the mark. But at the end of our talk he asked me why four particular BonBons were included in the book. (I won't identify them; maybe you can tell.)

I was stunned! Out of the 80 plus BonBons, those were the only ones I had written intentionally—from my head, rather than them coming to me in one fell swoop. How could he know?! How did he unerringly pick out the only four that did not arrive fully formed?

I had never shared that information with anybody—and assumed that nobody could ever tell the difference. But they'd been plunked out as not "tasting" like the others.

Those four BonBons looked like the rest, but somehow, *they didn't feel like the rest.* For Ross is attuned to binkles and upbeat energy enough to recognize that these particular ones didn't measure up. That doesn't mean they weren't helpful or good reading, but their energetic flavor wasn't right on.

A BonBon is three-centered, with something that speaks to our emotional, physical, and mental natures at the same time—and in perfect balance. But these had been too much mental—like a spice that is so heavy handed in a recipe that it fades out the other flavors.

I tell this story because Ross was resonating to the collection of BonBons with his heart. So, he could recognize those few that didn't speak to him in the same way. The heart identifies the authority of higher truth and "something more." So, he felt the letdown from those few which failed to resonate deeply.

Each of us has that same capacity, when we take the effort to give that awareness credence. That ability to tell the genuine from the look-alikes does not apply only to BonBons, but to anything we read or encounter that touches us deeply. Or fails to. The cliché or counterfeit wisdom stands out from the rest with a dull "thud."

I urge you to develop that capacity further. And to rely on it through thick and thin. It will not lead you wrong. As you read these BonBons, or other inspirational words, watch your own reaction for how you resonate to them.

- Can you taste the mental, the emotional, and physical threads in the message?

- Do you resonate within the appropriate part of yourself to each of them?

- Do you respond to them in a balanced way?

- Does your own wisdom leap forward in response?

That's what I hope these do for you.

BINKLE, KRINDLE, AND LAPHE WORK TOGETHER

To the concept of **binkles**, add two related notions: **krindle** and **laphe** (also coined by me).

- **Binkle** – the *energy* that is felt; the zizz, a moment of sensed perfection

- **Krindle** – the *meter* or battery within the body that detects and holds the special energy. It detects signs of available binkle energy in our surroundings, rather like a Geiger counter registers radiation

- **Laphe** – (pronounced, "laugh") the *sense of being full of binkles*; it acts as a balanced feeling that is centered within. Laphe acts as a self-adjusting shock absorber, but it is attuned to binkle energy. It keeps a person's upbeat energy level on an even keel. Laphe resembles the bubble in a level, indicating whether somebody's energy is balanced—"on the level" *or* "off kilter." When we're charged up and without stress, it provides a sense of fullness and happiness.

As you allow the binkle, krindle, and laphe to be engaged in responding to whatever is happening, you flow with the energetic currents that eddy around you. Like water, you're carried around life's rocky places.

Knowing that is a binkle indeed.

BONBONS—THE RECIPE

A BonBon is created when truth is pushed through a lens (an experience, a point of view, a personality), which then yields an insight.

In some way, each BonBon carries the messages:

- Life is designed to bring out the best in you.
- Be aware; be alive; be alert.
- Find the lesson and grow.
- There is a powerful message to be found in every event, every encounter.
- Enjoy whatever you do and, if possible, share it.
- People matter; kindness helps.
- You have more power and choices available than you realize or use.
- Resist your familiar and habitual reactions; try new responses.
- Life is precious; so are you.
- Self-discovery is the most challenging frontier, and there is never an end to it.
- Be grateful for the obstacles you encounter; use them to grow.
- There are many ways to see things and to respond to them; don't limit yourself.
- Pursue and enjoy the unexpected.
- Be an active force in your own life.
- Seek and accept your own wisdom.
- Truth becomes more real and complete for you each time you encounter it and respond to it without resistance.
- Find the fun, the humor inherent in everything that comes your way.

- What you *DO* is more important than what you think (though it reveals and reflects what you think).
- Continually challenge yourself to stay creative and fresh.

Experience the abundance of uplifting energy whenever you add BonBons to your daily diet. You can make some for yourself from the ingredients available to you in your own life. Your unique identity adds an additional delicious flavor. Receive something even better than truth—YOUR OWN TRUTH.

Remember, you can make a BonBon every time you push truth through your unique lens of awareness, through your identity, and discover an insight. Such insights are sure to nourish and enliven you.

Bon Appetit!

The box will never be empty, and neither will your life!

CHAPTER 2
DIVINITY—YOUR VISION AND DESTINY

Divinity has the lightness of a cloud—frothy, airy, translucent but slightly radiant—adding a gentle sweetness on the tongue. A bite of it is so effervescent it's out of this world—what we call "divine." How divine!

But that experience of lightness also brings a wisp of tranquility along. Divinity is the perfect food for the spirit as well as the taste buds. And it satisfies everything within that makes us feel lighthearted too.

The divinity of simplicity acts as an uplifting tonic for our too-hectic, too-burdened, roller coaster lives. But such sweetness can elevate our overall mood and outlook. It brings a respite from the denser, weightier, and demanding concerns that consume our tranquility.

Make it a priority to get enough sweetness, lightheartedness, and peaceful moments each day. Don't treat them as an afterthought—tucked in as catch-as-catch-can. Take time for a bite of divinity every chance you can.

- Opportunity Knocks
- Opportunity Knocks Again
- Opportunity Knocks—The Third Time
- Opportunity Knocks Yet Again
- Upholding a View
- The Guy Who Runs the Drawbridge
- In Praise of Blubbering and Yammering
- Port in the Norm
- Don't *Smell* the Roses
- I Wanna Have that Wanna-Happen Energy
- Down with Rules!
- Hope Is a Red Herring
- Blank Check
- Putting More Value on Values

Opportunity Knocks

Opportunity knocks—but not the way you expect. It doesn't come up to your door like a well-bred guest, asking for admittance. *Opportunity knocks you down.* As you lie there, feeling beaten, you have several choices:

- Fume and grumble—maybe even get angry
- Move on as quickly as possible and dismiss the whole thing
- Feel really bad about how this could have happened to you
- Try to figure out if it might be an opportunity being offered (actually, shoved at you)

When ambushed by adversity and disappointment, you are forced to see yourself and everything around you a little bit differently than usual. You get a chance to make a fresh start, set off in a new direction—coupled with the motivation to try it.

By knocking you down, something is trying very hard to get your attention. And the harder the whack, the more urgent is the message. Pay attention! You've been stopped, derailed, disconnected from your familiar routine.

So, pause a moment before moving on again. Take a good look at the people involved, the less-than-welcome situation, and the way it all relates to you. Notice intensely, giving attention to *all* the pieces. **It just might be opportunity knocking**.

Opportunity Knocks—Again

One way opportunity knocks is to knock you down to get your attention. Opportunity also knocks in a muffled and thumpy way. It keeps niggling at you, for a little while, just out of earshot, an intermittent ka-bump. It flirts with you, only to vanish as you attempt to listen harder.

But it returns—alluring but illusive.

If you ask someone else about it, they will strain and hear nothing. This is a summons just for you. It is for you alone to answer its beckoning—or dismiss it. It is as individual as a key to a lock. Actually, it is a key for your lock, but you won't know that unless you respond and pursue it.

Logic, good sense, and your existing commitments will feel no patience with such a wild goose chase. But if something in your nature is compelled to respond, you just might be able to grasp it.

At that moment, **opportunity becomes destiny!**

Opportunity Knocks—The Third Time

Opportunity sometimes knocks you down. Or it can lure you into seeking out what calls to your heart of hearts. But opportunity can also knock you solidly in the gut. Ugh!

We like to think of opportunity making us more likely to succeed. We imagine opportunity arriving in an intelligently-coherent way, with several attractive options. Assuming we like what's offered, we could go for it.

Hold on. That's not how opportunity works. It's not a business scheme, even a profoundly satisfying, long-term one. Something more significant is at stake, for opportunity relates to *the reason you're alive.*

The mortifying anguish that follows a major loss or disappointment knocks the stuffing out of you. Oomf! You're reeling and emptied out, and your confidence is nowhere to be found. The gnawing at the gut spawns despair and uncertainty—or is it the other way around?

Trust that! Don't deny it, avoid it, or put a pretty face on it. Don't look for blame or make excuses. Crashing to the bottom feels like having nowhere left to turn.

Wait... That's not the bottom. *That's precisely where opportunity hangs out.* At your darkest hour and within your deepest core resides something both real and solid that is *not defeated.* It's the side of yourself that transcends the finite and personal. It is not destroyed by life's setbacks, but rises above them.

Watch that power surge to the forefront—which seldom happens when life goes on as usual. Being flattened calls that quiet strength forward. Its presence resonates with clarity and new possibilities.

The door to untapped reserves and fresh beginnings is hidden on the other side of defeat. No wonder nobody intentionally seeks that route to success.

Being pummeled by circumstances may feel like all is lost. But perhaps something crucial is found. Opportunity knocks you into standing up with a fuller sense of yourself. It *sets free who you really are*, beyond the limits of personality. That's where trustworthy self-confidence resides.

Opportunity Knocks—Yet Again

Opportunity sometimes knocks every well-laid plan to pieces. Real opportunity is messy. It makes a shambles out of your elaborate intentions for the future. It upends your hopes and dumbfounds your assumptions.

But it also breaks down barriers that limit you and keep the brakes on. Such turmoil brings an abrupt re-shuffling of what *could* happen.

Along with the flash of disappointment comes a sensitivity to changing prospects. What was ignored in more stable times is now considered a godsend or a brilliant stroke of luck.

That reordering of possibilities also alters what you consider to be your strengths. You're being compelled to try new things and grow in entirely unfamiliar ways. Different or additional abilities will be called upon now—ones you're less confident about—ones never relied on before.

What follows disappointment and loss involves how to pick up the pieces. Consider the possibility that the broken plans and pieces scattered about are not the ones you should be picking up again.

What new paths or priorities are being opened up after it feels like all is lost? Look around for them, for they are waiting in the wings. How eager are you to seek them out?

Disruption also brings freedom. Not just *freedom from* what mattered to you before, but *freedom to* write your own ticket to something only dimly glimpsed.

Why not
- Make it grand in scope?
- Make it ambitious?
- Make it worthwhile?
- Make it satisfying?
- Make it uniquely yours?

The unblocked door that stands open briefly is called "Opportunity."

UPHOLDING A VIEW

My life is filled with many different kinds of people: family, professional colleagues, friends, close friends, nodding acquaintances, clients, audience members, people who provide me services, etc. In every case I offer and exchange different aspects of myself, providing different degrees of self-exposure or intimacy.

Recently, I have recognized a new category: *people I wish to uphold.* It has provided an entirely different way of looking at the people in my life, and it cuts across other existing roles and relationships. Being upheld is not a reflection of our closeness, how long we've known each other, or the kinds of needs they have. This category can't be applied to everyone with a need or I'd be consumed.

The coin is sincere caring and is paid in my time, energy, emotion, or even money. Upholding goes beyond the everyday display of encouragement and kindness. For whatever reason (and they are all so different), if I decide that "here is a person who *needs to be upheld,*" I create a one-sided commitment to him or her. I can just as easily and arbitrarily end it whenever I choose.

Although nothing needs to be said directly to the person, I feel obligated to find ways to uphold them and support their efforts. This special bond may not exist for long. The person may not even benefit from whatever I can do for long. But it exists as a priority for me until fulfilled.

Of course, such commitments make sense within the tight circle of family or intimate friends. But this relationship is different than those and may not even apply for anyone close. Those who are nearest to me might not be the ones who can use what is offered—offered freely, willingly and without strings. It doesn't establish a permanent arrangement. In fact, it's likely to be transitional, a bridge through painful, risky or discouraging times.

For example, a casual acquaintance decides to take a course required for a promotion, but lacks a ride, baby-sitter or whatever. By my providing the missing element, the person *and* their goal are both upheld.

My role in such a case is active and supportive, serving as a vote of confidence at a time when their effort seems daunting. The message is conveyed from me to them through kind words and deeds, "You're not alone in this. I'm here for you."

Or, you receive outstanding service from a small business struggling against well financed competition. In deciding to uphold the business, you not only patronize it but use your network of contacts to bring it new business. In being more than a customer, you're nourishing and rewarding the *values* that they display in how they serve you.

There's much more involved than spending money or even how well you might like the business owner. Through such supportive efforts you acknowledge and reward the behaviors you value.

Or, you decide to uphold a leader who's making hard, risky, or even unpopular decisions. In such a thankless role, the leader is vulnerable. Your decision to uphold them is really an acknowledgment of the guts or character necessary to achieve the desired goal. By your upholding stance, you're voting in a very tangible way for the preferred outcome.

From examining my ties to those who I've elected to uphold, I've found strengths and skills otherwise unused.

I've also discovered previously unnoticed ways in which others have been upholding me.

THE GUY WHO RUNS THE DRAWBRIDGE

There's a little guy up in your head who is in charge of attention. No matter what you had in mind, he (or she) is the one who really determines where your attention goes. His job is to run the mental drawbridge, which is opened when he's interested, and closed as soon as he loses interest.

He works long hours, but is very arbitrary about when to open or close the drawbridge. Since he stays in the background, most people don't even know he's there. Your mental gatekeeper is very powerful because that's who decides what you notice and respond to—and for how long.

The guy who runs the drawbridge:

- Has a short attention span and a poor memory— can't recall what else should be done now

- Loves to laugh—forgets other priorities and leaves the bridge down

- Is always on the lookout for variety, fun, excitement, and a good time

- Doesn't like sad or yucky stuff

- Is vain—prefers sincere flattery, recognition and praise, but will settle for any

- Shuts the bridge unexpectedly and without warning—especially when triggered by fears or old hurts

- Lacks any sense of proportion—often treating important matters as distractions, but trivial ones as significant

- Can be lured away from where his attention should be by curiosity or any bright and shiny thing

- Responds in kind and intensity to those who touch him emotionally—for good or ill

- Is impressed by (and responds to) status and name dropping

- Is easily frightened or bored, so forgets to stay alert or on task

NOTE: See also, The Problem D'Solver Laws, Chapter 6

*This image is the registered trademark ® of Faith Lynella, The Problem D'Solver
   Slogan: *Every problem is an invitation to open your mind and your heart*

In Praise of Blubbering and Yammering

Everyone experiences life in three ways—logically, emotionally and physically. Early on, we learned to let the logical side do the talking. It's good at it and people are more likely to pay attention.

Since our logical side controls the mouth it assumes it calls the shots. But it edits out information that doesn't make sense to it—information that isn't rational. What it deletes is primarily related to the body and emotions.

When our emotional side tries to speak up and be "logical" it blubbers. When our physical side tries to speak up and be "logical" it yammers. Neither of which comes across as articulate—but that doesn't mean the body and emotions don't have anything worth saying.

Neither blubbering (hurt feelings) nor yammering (body hurts) come across as persuasive or coherent. To the extent their message gets through at all, it's likely to be embarrassing for both the speaker and the listener. The point is almost always lost because it's made so ineptly.

Our logical side wants to leap in and tidy up the information since it, too, doesn't "get it." That's why the blubbering or yammering started in the first place.

So, here's the dilemma—whether to persist with belaboring the issue that's putting you in a poor light, or to drop it—let it go, resolved to "forget the whole thing."

When it comes to verbal expression the body and emotions are woefully inept—they're accustomed to keeping quiet. So, when they do speak out—however awkwardly—pay attention. Listen. Trust there's something being said that your logical mind didn't notice or can't address. But it's something you need to be aware of, nonetheless.

Respect the sincerity of what's being expressed, however illogically. Don't attempt to turn it off. Listen beyond the words, for the underlying message.

Muzzle your own smooth-talking logical point of view that's eager to edit or correct. Consider the blubbered or yammered information relevant, since there's a core of truth in it—truth that would be so easy to ignore.

It takes courage to let yourself blubber or yammer. It takes even more courage to listen and respect the perplexing message. Yet you'll be amazed by what you'll discover about yourself on those channels you've assumed carried only gibberish or static.

Tune it in, don't tune it out.

Don't *Smell* the Roses

"Stop and smell the roses." How often have you heard that one? Please don't just smell them. There's so much more to be experienced—a world untapped in every blossom.

Discover a totally new relationship with flowers, the stuff of nature, or whatever is around you that's seldom noticed or appreciated. Start by *deciding to notice*. Make what's usually in the background of your busy life front and center. Pay attention, now. Focus the full horsepower of your sensory apparatus on a single flower, for instance.

Hold on. Wait... don't rush this.

What do your **eyes see**? Shift magnification, noting shades of light and shadow, the colors, the textures, the closed still-unpopped buds, the wobble in the breeze, its rootedness into the earth, the bugs crawling on the stem or buzzing around it.

Touch it—gently now. Is it warm from the sun? Moist from the dew? Do the bloom and leaves gently yield to your fingers, while being springy on the bud, yet tough and resisting in the stem? Can you imagine how much more a blind person would be "seeing" with their touch?

Listen. A flower may be silent, but it grows in a world that's anything but. Bend down—eye to eye, ear to bloom, with it. Stand still, your ear as close as possible. Get quiet, really

really quiet. Turn off the hum of mental chatter, your personal Muzak.

Can you hear the flower now? The buzz of insects, the chirp of birds, the rustling of the wind in nearby branches, the purposeful footsteps of someone going by, the hum of traffic in the distance. You might even hear the rubbing of the fabric in your clothes as you breath in and out. Quiet? No way!

OK, *now* **smell it**. Really do it right, with your eyes closed—slow and deep. Don't just smell the blossom, but also the leaves, buds, seedpods, noting how the various parts seem the same—and different.

Compare the part that's in the sun with the same part that's in shadow. Is it mustier? Crush a leaf or a petal and inhale the essence released. Let your mind run free. What associations come bubbling up? Are you transported back to grandmother's garden? What emotions flood in?

Taste it. Knowing that some plants are poisonous, think twice about chewing and swallowing. Build on what your nose unlocked. Is the taste familiar? Like an herb? Bursting with succulent life force?

Roll it around in your mouth and explore its texture with the tongue, against the lips. Notice all the associations and emotions unleashed. Drag it out.

Five senses—infinite observations. And that's just the beginning—that's the flower as each sense takes it in. Now step back (physically and mentally) so you can experience the whole flower with the whole of you. Doesn't awe and wonder bubble up? Don't you, for a moment, feel the magic of "seeing" like a young child? There are no ideas about the flower—just the enjoyment of it, as you respond to its delicate beauty.

Take a quick check out of the corner of your eye, in the back of your mind. Life's problems are nowhere to be found—for the moment. They're eclipsed by the splendor of a flower, along with your taking the time to put something else ahead of them.

That's just one flower, but an encounter very worth your time. It's one that every flower offers—and any object that's experienced sincerely can provide.

THE PORT IN THE NORM

All day every day, from the time you arise, you face non-stop demands: notice me, feed me, invest in me, read me, buy me, water me, remember me, answer me. From all directions, they tug at you with relentless and insistent voices. Dealing with them all is the norm. Doesn't it ever stop? Is it possible to ever do enough to still the clamoring?

Whether the source is inanimate (fold me, put me away, pay me) or animate (play with me, love me, walk me), whether external (make dinner, service the car) or internal (frustrations about something forgotten or a lapse of kindness), you are under siege.

Surrounded from every side with non-stop cries for your attention and energy, there is no relief to be found. Even with the greatest willingness to please, you are overwhelmed. There is only one place to turn that is not prey to the unrest.

Go deep within—to the quiet place that always waits your visit. You have a serene sanctuary, safe from the buffeting of outrageous events. Relax, treasure the tranquility of your own quiet place. Time itself stands still while you do so.

As your judgment clears, you temporarily discover that those demanding voices cannot touch you. Whatever you sink into while there renews and protects you. It is not diminished by the pressures of the world.

Become a timeless traveler, and escape the strident, unrelenting calls that leave you no peace. As you explore the sanctuary of your own unpressured wisdom, you travel to the *port in the norm*.

I WANNA HAVE THAT WANNA-HAPPEN ENERGY

Once in a while, a project or idea comes together of its own accord. It's so seamless, spontaneous, and rapid I just have to hang on. There's a singleness of purpose that pushes aside whatever else competes for my time, attention, or energy. Something in me recognizes "it's got a mind of its own." What it is trying to accomplish is counter-intuitive, which means I wouldn't have thought to do that in a million years.

Wanna-Happen Energy puts me in unresisting overdrive. This is Clear Sailing Energy, but riding on a schooner instead of a dinghy. It takes over my Do List. But it doesn't stay there long because what needs doing is so quickly accomplished. Then the whole thing is off to what's next, because it *wants to happen*. If it joins up with the buoyancy of Lift-off Energy, there could be a game-change. Things really start to move!

The energetic surge pulls me right along. Yet this process isn't hurried so much as incredibly efficient. Unerringly, no thought or motion is wasted or off-track. I get even more oomph from doing the work—without feeling drained at all. I'm energized! I'm almost giddy about *getting to do it* because it feels like such a privilege to be involved.

This state of affairs resembles a blueprint just waiting to be made tangible—no trial and error or fumbling around. Somehow, on some level, it's apparent this isn't half-baked or a pile of unrelated pieces. But it exists as a whole, with just a bit of assembly required of me.

This is not Breakthrough Energy since there are no barriers or logjams to be breached. Nothing stands in its way. The force of it overrides existing everyday rhythms and routines, as it proceeds toward its driving purpose.

You feel a rush of joy and delight as Wanna-Happen Energy is going on. But after it passes there's a saddened letdown. Not yet!... Oh no... is it over?! You realize that whatever just happened was an event—something special to be pondered and reflected upon. But wondering about the hows and whys can't explain it—or bring it back.

That burst of vitalizing energy didn't arise from you, but you gladly played your part. Now your role is to watch with reverent appreciation to see what comes of it. What will bloom from it? How far will that impulse go? Whatever it brings will defy logic or staid expectations.

While it wasn't of your making, you can't help wishing that glorious Wanna-Happen Energy can stick around longer, or can come back again soon.

DOWN WITH RULES!

I really do not like rules. Their proliferation in every aspect of life is the legacy of our infatuation with logic—as well as doomed attempts to be absolutely clear. It starts with a few rules. But then, more rules are needed to clear up what wasn't quite clear enough. And the madness continues. Every rule is an assault on judgment.

Reliance on rules replaces judgment and principled choices, which are much more important in how we conduct our affairs. Worshiping rules for their own sake ignores both qualities—and that fixation has cost us dearly. Conforming to external rules undermines a person's responsibility for the way they behave.

The emphasis has shifted from making choices rooted in good judgment and common sense to picking our way through a world of narrowly defined rules. Too often, people treat anything that's not against the rules as fair game—acceptable.

So, the challenge becomes, how close can you come to violating the rules without crossing the line or getting caught? The result: ever more equally foolish and short-sighted choices. As common sense has been devalued, it's become downright scarce.

Yet a part of myself is aware of something more important than conforming to official rules and regulations. I can sense the calling of my higher nature, toward those values we all have in common. Those transcend nit-picky rules—and should not be sacrificed to them.

Unquestioned, blind compliance also erodes honor, which has little effect unless it's rooted in a person's values and character. Every one of us has been diminished by a system that rewards mindless obedience to external standards that far exceed courtesy and fair play. Such conduct is at the expense of responsible behavior that grows out of integrity and good judgment.

Down with Rules! Up with Judgment!

Hope Is a Red Herring

Hope—how we cling to it in times of crisis, and when the risks are high. We hope we'll make it through, and that help is on the way. Then in trivial matters we continue to hope—that the phone will (or won't) ring, that the car will start, that the check will clear. What is hoped for often seems beyond your control, somehow. But still you keep hoping.

Hope, hope, hope. It gets linked up with all those things we want to happen. So, we hope and wait, living in a state of unsatisfied expectancy. That's not the same as being open to what is *already happening*, or being receptive to whatever is to come.

Hope blinds us to both of them and sets us up for disappointment. It makes us discontented with what's in hand here and now, choosing to dream and expect something different. Keeping your eyes ever on the future puts more store in *what might happen* than on what is actually occurring.

Hope is akin to confident anticipation (savoring something expected in advance) and creative visualization (holding a specific goal in mind until it's achieved). While they're not the same, any of the three can too easily make you passive in the face of the very involved role you could play. Hoping is often impatient for what you desire (or think you deserve).

Anything worth hoping for is worth pursuing actively. Elevate a hope to be more than a daydream, a wouldn't-it-be-nice-if… Turn it into a firm goal that you're ready to commit to make a reality. Make the desired outcome as concrete as you know how. Take the preparatory steps toward reaching it—baby steps or giant steps, any steps will do.

Add a dose of resolve and a full-bodied heave ho. Already what you've been yearning for is a step closer to reality. Hope is OK when it's backed up with effort—but not enough to carry the day.

Do something about what you hope will happen right now. Plant seeds and tend them. **Act like it's all up to you and fate may lend a hand**. Taking *tangible action* puts you into the equation, and that's miles ahead of wistfully hoping that what you want will happen.

BLANK CHECK

What's the value of a blank check?

That's up to you.

You fill in the amount, rather than it being done by the person whose bank account it is written upon. Large or small—the size of the dollar figure entered is entirely in your hands—just as you decide how and where you spend it. The amount you fill in is exactly *as large as your expectations or vision.*

What stops you from making the amount absurdly large?

- Certainty that for some reason the check won't clear—that there's nothing to draw upon

- Doubt that you'll get what you ask, or a wariness there's a trick somehow

- Reluctance to be greedy, to expect too much; it seems unfair, to not think you're worth it

- Hesitation to reach for a brass ring—especially considering prior disappointments

- Suspicion that you're being played for a sucker— it couldn't be *that* good

- Distractions that focus your attention elsewhere— missing the boat entirely

Your life is a blank check. It's drawn on the unlimited resources of the Bank of Infinite Possibilities. Whatever amount you write in, *it will clear.* Its value to you keeps expanding as you spend it, fulfilling your hopes and desires. All you desire can be yours for the taking. What it's worth to you depends on what you do with it.

Think vast—consider *what could be*. Function expansively. Give generously. Don't think small or safe. Why not see how far your blank check can take you?

PUTTING MORE VALUE ON VALUES

Values don't come neatly packed in a box. Nor are they like emergency supplies, tucked away for a crisis—forgotten until all else fails. Neither are they one-size-fits-all since the ones that apply particularly to you must be developed and tested over a lifetime.

Despite all the talk about the need for a renewal of values, they are not taken very seriously in this "get what you can" world. They're certainly not very close to the front of the line when it comes to most people's priorities.

Ideals and behavior go together—or not. And they are expensive because the values that truly matter only come at the expense of easier, more self-centered, and more practical choices. Our values are a byproduct of character. Both have to be built by making themselves tangible through one choice at a time, one deliberate act at a time— over and over again. Even when it doesn't seem to count.

Letting our values guide us requires us to put something (or someone) else first. Values are those intangible principles you prize enough to aspire to them, seek them out, hold them dear. But never doubt that *you give them their value* whenever you hold them aloft as more than a good idea. *You* make them a force in the world by how you act in accord with them.

Values are a part of the "what could be" that shines a beckoning light to guide your feet. Letting them influence your behavior can protect you from who-knows-how-many errors in judgment. Your inner self is nourished when worthwhile values are engaged, and diminished when they are absent.

Yes, living from and through your values can be challenging. It's nearly impossible at times—but even the attempt to do so is still a worthy pursuit, come what may. You should keep them in the picture (no matter which priorities prevail in the end). But that struggle to live your values is not nearly as difficult as having to live without them.

Chapter 3
Jellies—Fun and Fruity

BonBons are "the good stuff" of life. The French word as Good-Good signifies an indulgence, a reward, a step above ordinary nourishment. A sweet BonBon makes you pause and savor the moment a tad longer. So good... So delicious... So worth lingering over...

BonBons can be lighthearted and playful, as well as laden with wisdom. Yet each of them speaks of worthy and sometimes timeless matters. But that doesn't mean they have to be ponderously serious. The profound can be enjoyable and upbeat too. Each BonBon can feed the spirit—with a tantalizing flavor that lingers long after.

These nourish the playful side of yourself—the innocent and guileless child who never gets old, or jaded, or resigned. Nourish that spirit since it has the capacity to find joy everywhere. And it keeps us amused and engaged.

So, relish these BonBons as a tangy treat that can make your life even more delicious. Feel the uplifting rise in mood as your youthful spirits rise. Remember every BonBon has a high-energy center.

- Alligator Watch
- "I Can Make You a Star"
- Get the Joke
- Be the Kind Kind
- Love Letter to a Cat
- What Makes God Happy?
- The Heart Cannot Do Math
- Open until Filled...
- Clumsy Is Glorious!
- Snappy Jolly Days
- The Joy of Joy
- Changing Gears on the Sly

ALLIGATOR WATCH

*When you're up to your ass in alligators, it's hard
to remember you came to drain the swamp.*
Author Unknown

Sometimes alligator attacks seem like they'll go on forever.
No sooner have you dealt with one crisis, then there's
another, then another, then another. Each attack insists on
being taken seriously and handled NOW. Alligators seem
to come in bunches—triumph over one and there are many
more in line.

When beset by the need to bail a sinking boat or solve a
crisis, speed and endurance are critical. Your ability to do
anything the "right" way, let alone the "carefully planned"
way, is a routine casualty.

The assaults that come with living in crises mode are
draining and soul deadening. "If I can just get through
this, then..."

Anything that's less urgent gets pushed into "then...." Life
as you'd like to live it inevitably goes on "hold." If you dare
to wonder "How much more can I take?" you needn't wait
long to find out.

Fortunately, such trials help us to find strengths seldom
used and to discover what matters most. The need to find

"those things that endure" becomes paramount. Trivialities fall away, and you get to find out who your true friends are. Such discoveries are the upside of the downside.

As you drag on, enduring, struggling, fending off whatever form the alligator of the moment takes, what could possibly seem like progress? As long as there's yet another alligator, you're vulnerable to their persistent influence. You can be pulled into the fray repeatedly—rather than rising above it.

Take heart—look at what you've been through, and survived, and discovered (although the value of that comes later, in a more reflective mode).

Recognize the swamp is a bit less swampy. And the original goal is not as far off as it was.

Notice, too, you're now only up to your knees in alligators. Can ankles be far behind?

"I Can Make You a Star"

Why do we so willingly get swept into some movies and books? We become deeply involved with the characters, their lives and their concerns. We get inside their skins and feel their emotions, as we experience their hopes and frustrations almost first-hand. We know our favorites' thoughts so well we can anticipate what they'll think and say next.

A good author or director invites that degree of involvement. That imaginary world seems to be tangible enough and engaging enough for us to temporarily step into it. We feel we belong there. We care so much about those people and their world it hurts to leave them.

As we suspend our disbelief, we forget it's only a work of fiction—a world created to entertain or inform (if it is a real person's life). That other world seems so real while we're immersed in it that it's not just an escape. We're alert to our surroundings, the prevailing mood, and the many subtle signals that build upon each other.

All our senses were engaged—at the ready. Our reactions to the events and people encountered need to be appropriate and novel for being there. (See why works of fiction are called novels?)

Next time, notice your frame of mind *as you return from that fictional world*, as you step back to your own life. You can briefly view the world you inhabit as an interloper because you've been outside of it—in the other landscape. Functioning with somebody else's mindset.

Quickly, before you become blind to this freedom from your familiar ways of seeing and responding to your everyday existence, ponder thoughts like these:

1. Think of your own life as a movie in which you are both the director and star (you are, you know). You can as fully enjoy the scenes of your movie as anything at the cinema or on the printed page. Crank up your senses and notice how much more vivid what happens to you can be when given your full attention.

2. Get to know the characters in your life in more detail. That's not knowing their factual details, but takes a 360 degree look that sees somebody beyond the externals. Is it time to write in some new and different parts, add some new characters? Or how about writing out certain characters? Or how about dialing back the conflict, drama, or suspense?

3. Why not alter some scenes? Stretch some of them out and abbreviate others. Give more time to the experiences that are most touching, pleasant, or emotionally rewarding for you, while collapsing those full of pain, frustration, or tedium. Never forget that you have the ability to re-write your own behavior as your priorities change. Or as you get better at reading the signals.

4. Notice your own ebbs and flows of energy, your ups and downs, the shifts in your mood and attention. You are free to detach from them in the same way you can observe the moods of fictional characters. Try caring about yourself in the same positive ways that you feel toward your favorite characters.

   But here's a major difference between your life and works of fiction (or non-fiction when the real people aren't you). You can also be *aware of yourself being yourself.* So, you get to see the particular scene both from the inside (your usual view) and from the outside (as the director or viewer would see it).

5. Drama and excitement don't exist in the events by themselves. Those emotional reactions arise through the way we choose to experience them. Nothing in fiction could be as dramatic, as intense, as climatic, or as fulfilling as the ongoing scene you walk through day by day. You just need to tune into your own life fully. Become more engaged—and stay engaged.

Your life is like a great movie, full of interesting characters, unique plot twists, sensuous details, moments of aching beauty or pain, and recurring themes across a span of years. And talk about suspense in the plotting... Tomorrow is always a cliffhanger because you never can be sure what's just around the corner...

You're the star! So, why not make your life a productive work of art? Living your life is your art; it's who you art. So why not give your life's drama four bright stars?

GET THE JOKE

God is a practical joker. He loves pratfalls, slapstick, and pie-in-the-face humor. God enjoys puns and conundrums and riddles of all sorts, laying out elaborate schemes that end in "Gotcha!" He hides his presence in obscure and paradoxical ways, leaving oblique clues that could help to track him down. (That's God playing hide and seek with us.)

This is the playful and comic side of the infinite, who will go to any length for a laugh, or a titter, or a groaner.

God delights in playfulness and joy—where children are miles ahead of the serious-minded. God wants to romp and play, always on the lookout for enthusiastic playmates. He hopes that we can discover the fun, the momentary uncertainty before we land in the mud hole, as well as the novelty of experiences that blow up in our faces, that we otherwise treat as reliable.

You can count on the Infinite to take potshots at our pompous certainty that we are in control or know what to do.

So, your path is littered with banana peels. Sooner or later we slip, landing on our faces, setting the stage for a sobering moment. The next instant the universe hangs in anticipation... waiting for your reaction... You explode with laughter or anger—go up or go down with the experience.

God waits... hoping... eager to know, "Did you get it? Did you get my joke? Can you find the humor in this?" In that ever-so-brief moment, God *waits for you.*

Slapstick humor depends on there being a fall guy. So, when you've "taken the fall" without taking it personally, you get to be *in on the joke*. Sure, it hurts like heck. It wounds your pride—but it's funny all the same. When you can laugh at yourself and see the humor of your downfall, you're saying "I get it!"

And in that moment, *God laughs with you*—and you can spot the wink.

BE THE KIND KIND

Life need not be complicated:
  When in doubt—Be kind.
  When *not* in doubt—Be kind.

When difficulties abound like a swarm of gnats, taking your frustration out on those around you won't make your situation better. Only worse—less caring.

When life seems like a mucky muddle—devoid of purpose—there's no good that comes from blaming or complaining. From dropping the ball.

All the philosophies and religious principles in the world are mere lip service if they don't make us more caring people. Just because it's tough to do... or rejected... or misunderstood... or seems to be futile...

That's no excuse. No excuse at all! It's still what needs doing—all the more so.

Kindness rebuilds the whole, indifferent world—one thoughtful gesture at a time. Challenge by challenge. Person by person. Moment by moment. Isn't that enough?!

Stick with it—Or you'll be AWOL – Absent Without Love

LOVE LETTER TO A CAT

Dear Miss Puss,

I love the gentle way you insist upon being at the center of my desk as I attempt to work around you—making it plain what's really important here.

I love the way you can turn anything into an object for play and then explore its endless possibilities.

I love the way you refuse to notice my call and then come in stealthily as soon as you think it is your idea.

I love the attentive and rapt way you watch the tiniest details, ready to engage or pounce in a flash.

I love the way you gaze down from high places, the regal sovereign of all you survey.

I love the way you make yourself vulnerable to me, displaying how totally you trust me, rely on me, and want me to care about nothing but you.

I love the way you seek out visitors (selected by some criteria that only you can detect) for special attention—

instant and total devotion—and then, as arbitrarily, dismiss them.

I love the way you shift so abruptly from languid inertia to dynamic speed, and then as quickly go back to laziness again.

I love the way you embody gracefulness in every movement—as you thrust out a paw, yawn with all of your being, and sink into a mound of fur.

In these and many other ways you remind me:

- That my routine practical obligations are not that important
- That life can be fun, dynamic and ever-fresh
- That curiosity is well rewarded with marvelous discoveries
- That devotion is a precious gift
- That it is possible to meet events on my own terms
- That play is always an available choice—and not a waste of time
- That it is wise to be alert for unexpected pleasures
- That resting is an art form
- That simple is enough

What Makes God Happy?

I'm fed up with all the religious doctrines telling us what you Must Do or Must Not Do in order to have a relationship with God. It's as though those who speak in his name know what hoops you need to jump through to make God happy.

Principled behavior matters—matters very much. But that depends on virtuous living and developing character and good judgment. Those work with or without a belief in God.

But you don't need to act like a well-trained dog who knows how to jump through all the hoops in order to feel the presence of God in your life.

To those with all the rules I say, "Hogwash!" What makes God happy is *you being happy*, and kind, and full of joy. But if you want a list, I'll give you one. I'm willing to tell you what pleases God, and there's no dogma required to score 100%. Or make your own list—as long as every item on it can make you feel this way.

- Being happy now—not someday, not when such-and-such happens. Right here; right now

- Appreciating the world and all the rich diversity to be found in it: natural beauty, mind-boggling, "how can that be?", or experiences that take your breath away

- Letting love and caring trump your habitual ways of relating to others or getting things done

- Seeing life through the eyes of a child, with curiosity and innocence

- Taking the time to care deeply about each other—kindly, openly, without strings attached, and with great respect for who the other person is

- Being kind to yourself—the loving side of yourself being directed to the side that's hungry for it

- Picking yourself up with gladness in your heart for all you learned by the fall

How do I know?

Behavior like this makes me well up with a fullness that tells me all is well, that there is a rightness beyond what seems to be so painful. To me, that sensation reminds me that I'm in the presence of God. Acts like these have been known to work wonders.

But you can make your own list of experiences in which you know that sensation with every fiber of your being.

And that's how you can tell, too.

NOTE: The above cartoon was created by Nick Newberry and me as part of our Cloudside Chats series of cartoons.

THE HEART CANNOT DO MATH

The heart doesn't keep score or play tit-for-tat. Rather, it is driven by joy and the emotional rewards that can be found almost anywhere. It searches for what is beautiful and graceful, for that gladdens the soul. The heart knows the best things in life are free—or impossible to put a price tag on.

The heart cares much more about a person's values and character, for it is attuned to what abides beyond our practical concerns. It cares, and cares deeply. It is unconcerned about them-versus-us or you-versus-me considerations, but considers it a given that we are all fundamentally similar, members of a larger whole.

The heart is inspired to act on benevolent impulses that put the pressing concerns of others first, to step in and lend a hand or provide a kind word where it's needed. It does so without stopping to wonder, What's in it for me? It reaches out to the dispirited or vulnerable, providing what their hearts want as well—love and recognition.

The heart shares what it has, even beyond what's reasonable. It acts spontaneously to extend a hand or to try to make a difference. It makes no distinction between dealing with a particular person's problem that needs attention and serving the world at large. For it is blind to scale or the risk of long odds.

The heart is generous and spontaneous, less interested in what *could* happen eventually than *what needs to happen now.* Some would claim that approach makes the heart short-sighted, for it acts in the heat of the moment. But it acts from a virtuous purpose and it does not doubt.

The heart happily forgives a wrong done to us, without extracting a pound of flesh. That's getting into math. It doesn't know how to hold a grudge. Nor can it imagine why it should.

Some might think that listening to the heart makes us a sucker for lost causes and foolhardy aims, as we set out to right the sorrows and pain that seem to never end. But it hears the beckoning of our higher angels, and cannot turn away.

The heart envisions a better future for all—if we can just put aside our secondary differences and pull together. If each of us can bring our unique and best efforts to the task. It even keeps feeling that way, no matter how often it turns out differently.

The brain is the side of us that does the math—that wants to evaluate and compare, to plan, and to split hairs in order to decide what's valuable. Whereas, the heart lacks the capacity to reduce life's precious moments to cost-versus-benefit analysis, or to calculate the risks. Trust the mind to figure all that out. That's its strength.

However, the heart can feel pain, grief, loss, and cruelty as well—not just the sunny emotions. It longs to remain open, even when risky or doing so invites abuse. So, it is not good at protecting itself. The head does a much better job of that. And that's where its ability to do math, and assess risks, and fight back come into play.

But sometimes the brain is willing to stand back in awed restraint when love and caring are front and center. That's the heart's work. Fortunately, every one of us has both a brain and a heart. And they work best as a team. And when they work together, that ensures each of us is at our best too.

Open Until Filled…

It's too late to be the first person in the world—that's been done. And it's not possible to be the only person in the world—there are too many others. But it's not too late to be the best YOU in the world. In fact, the job is yours— undisputed job security.

It's not a part-time, temporary position. It's one that grows with you. Variety? You bet, as much as you want. Travel? If you want. On the job training? The only kind—and you're not locked into a single career track. The sky's the limit!

Opportunity to take initiative? Goes with the territory. Benefits? Whatever you require—just ask. Promotions? Sure, why not? While you never get to stop being yourself, how you see yourself, and what you're capable of, will surely change with time and experience.

Time off? Depends on how you prefer to spend your time. It's your call. Replaced by a machine? No way! Outsourced or the work shipped overseas? Can't happen.

You, and only you, are the sole candidate for the YOU position.

Congratulations, the job is yours! Make of it what you will. It's the work of a lifetime—with more at stake than a pension plan.

CLUMSY IS GLORIOUS!

How I laughed and jumped into the air! I twisted and bounded in all directions. I gathered speed and leapt higher, with all the ease of a ballerina. And all the time I was shouting: "I'm clumsy! I'm clumsy! I'm clumsy!"

I need only say "I'm clumsy" to have the entire joyous experience come rushing back to me. In that sense of fleet-footedness I was not the least bit awkward, but grace personified. Inside, I was soaring, unfettered, buoyant, shorn of limits—a truly free spirit.

How ironic the event arose because I discovered I am clumsy. The evidence had been there all my life. There are perennial bruises on my hips since I so frequently bump them in doorways and against furniture.

My exercise regime consists of picking up things I knock over or drop. But for all those years I preferred not to see the pattern, treating each inelegant example as an isolated case.

Whatever awkward (talk about an ungainly word) event triggered that effervescent outburst was no different than a hundred others before—not a big deal in itself. What set it apart was, I saw it without judging and rejecting myself in that split-second.

This time I noticed—without making any excuses or feeling diminished by what happened. Being clumsy was simply a fact—it is true. I recognized both the truth of it and that it didn't matter. It was OK. I was OK!

I allowed myself to look directly at a long-denied reality about myself. I accepted the "wart" and loved myself no less for having it. In fact, I glimpsed the little girl I've always been and recognized that in every case where I felt clumsy I didn't like myself very much; I'd shrink inside. But that day, I did! I loved the oft-rejected, awkward, bumbly side of myself who could finally bask in the undeniable truth of it.

In that dual self-awareness and self-acceptance, I undid a lifetime of hurt. It erased the restraining fallout (haha) from the clumsy acts themselves. Even more, I lovingly embraced that little girl who bore the weight of that rejection. Indeed! Clumsy is glorious!

Snappy Jolly Days*

The word "holiday" started as a "holy day" with religious significance. I like to consider them as "whole-e days"—when we take a break from our labors in order to celebrate—to be wholly engaged and happy. As we're surrounded with warm family and friends we can feel united and whole.

Each holiday is a day of celebration and recognition. For me, part of the importance of the day is finding a new and personal way to relate to it. Try making variations in the way you say them that acknowledge the particular holiday, yet give it an additional message.

Re-christen a jolly-day to make it uniquely yours. (Say these out loud.)

New Year's Day   Slew of Cheers Day—Hooray! Hooray! Hooray!

Memorial Day   Remember It All Day—Pause and be grateful for what you both shared

Columbus Day   Call on Us Day—Visit a seldom seen friend; Discover their world

4th of July   More for Your Life—Celebrate! You're free!

Mother's Day   Mom Hears Day—She listens to

74

our hearts today and every day

Father's Day   Pa Steers Day—He guides our
                            way, our steps

Labor Day   Savor Day—Enjoy whatever
                            happens and play with abandon

Thanksgiving Day That's Living! Day—Full of food,
                            closeness, and a sense of
                            gratitude

Christmas Day   Kissed Most Day—Give affection
                            as well as receive it

Valentine's Day   Pal of Mine Day—I care about
                            you and acknowledge we're
                            connected (not just romantic)

Washington's Birthday Watching 'em (in
                            government); make authorities
                            recall they serve us

Lincoln's Birthday   Linking up mirth way—Join
                            together; make friends; laugh

Veteran's Day   Better Ones Day—They did
                            good for all of us; that matters

King Day   More than Kin Day—Embrace
                            everyone, every day; see how
                            we're alike

*This is an example of frivel, inspired wordplay, where there
are additional meanings to be decoded from the words
themselves. (See Frivel in Chapter 1.)

THE JOY OF JOY

Over my sink hangs a plaque, "The Natural State of Man is Joy." I see it daily. And sometimes it makes me pause before I get caught up in another errand. Where's the joy?

Who's got time for that? It doesn't even make the "To Do" list. How did I forget to treat being joyful as deserving of my time and energy? Rather, I've treated joy like a guilty indulgence, a forbidden pleasure, a truancy from responsibility.

It's time for a reality check. I'm determined to have lots more joy in my life—which means minimizing those activities (and people) preventing me from having it.

I want joy more than things, more than leisure, more than respect—because none of that will suffice without a full dollop of happiness and joy. Along with joy comes delight and gladness—worthy reprieves from the dull routines that gobble up the hours.

It's not that hard to have all the joy we want. It rubs up against us like a cat at the ankles, begging to be noticed. It does its best to sneak into the "important" things we struggle to make "perfect"—unless we wall it out as an untimely distraction.

Resistance to joy can be considered another name for stress. As our joy goes up, our stress level goes down. And vice versa. Give yourself permission to embrace the joyful buoyancy and all that comes with it at every opportunity.

Revel in the freedom it brings. Let its influence ooze into more weighty matters. Pause to enjoy each crumb encountered. Savor it, dawdle over it, taste how it feels—deeply and slowly.

Surrender to joy. Let it invade those jealously-hoarded minutes. It only adds to their value. There is no shame, no guilty secret revealed if we can embrace the joy of joy. The shame is when we don't. When life is hard and the unbidden thought comes, "What is it all for?"

The answer is, For Joy! For Joy!

Note: My mother had three daughters. She gave us each a special gift in her choosing our middle names, for it came to shape our character:

- Lynella Faith*
- Madelon Grace
- Geneva Joy

Although Joy came last (the youngest), it fulfills the others—Faith and Grace. But together it's an unbeatable combination.

*I changed my name to Faith Lynella (while omitting my last name). That decision arose from the discovery that for me "Faith" cannot come second. I have to lead **from** faith and **as** Faith.

The mind is mighty sneaky. There's not much chance of making it do something major it doesn't want to do. We think we can. Ha ha, that's the joke! It *lets us think* we're doing, and thinking, and actively pursuing exactly what we'd intended. We go merrily along, seldom noticing the extent to which what we *intend to do* and what we *actually do* have so little to do with each other.

So, your ready-to-change self needs to be equally devious in order to bring about desired changes. Especially if they are disruptive, go in a very different direction, or mess with our usual self-reward system. Success could well depend on sneaking the new behavior past the old guard, who doesn't want anything to be altered.

At its core, any attempt to make behavior change is taking on the *status quo*. Don't forget who you're up against— your unacknowledged self, who's really pulling your strings from behind the curtain.

Loose lips sink hips.
Don't make a big deal about it. Set the goal quietly in motion. Why do dieters so frequently fail? They'd rather talk about their diet plans, talk about food, talk about their goals than using their mouths for something else— not eating.

1. Take tiny baby steps, but lots and lots of them.
Just do something *a little bit differently*, then change another detail, then another. But not by much. Start making tiny changes to almost anything you do habitually. Interfere with habits since they are the guardians of inertia and "leave well enough alone."

So many seemingly inconsequential disturbances in routine won't bring out the big guns of resistance.

2. Make illogical connections, leaps, and feints.

The unexpected, but abrupt and "off target" move often achieves more than careful planning could. Drop. Break. Lose. Blunder. They work because they break continuity then take advantage of the chaos. Let random be your friend for a while. Back into your new behavior by chaotic misdirection.

3. Inject some playfulness.

Unless you can find a way to make the new behavior pleasant and fun, it's really hard to stick with it very long. Especially when it's all uphill. Lightheartedness adds breathing space and recharges the energy needed to carry on during the transition.

4. Involve another person who wants the same thing.

Helping and encouraging each other makes both of you stronger, more determined, more resilient. Also, the extraordinary effort needed that you couldn't tap into for yourself can often be done to benefit someone you care about.

5. Change the stakes.

When you can arrange for there to be *more rewards for making a change* (and going forward with a dream) than there are for leaving things as they are, things do change. Remember, there are powerful incentives to leave a situation the way it is—even an uncomfortable one. Don't forget to dismantle those kinds of rewards too.

6. Make a mess of it.

Let the stuck situation get even worse, so disordered and "broken" there's no putting it back together like before. That makes it easier to go ahead toward the beckoning goal than to attempt to go back. That's akin to burning your own bridges so you can't retreat.

Many things are going to be changing in your life, and all around you. The question to be faced is whether you want to be influencing and directing where it's headed? Or are you opting to be stuck forever in a catch-up mode?

NOTE: See Ligatures of Devotion, Chapter 5.

Chapter 4

Soft Centers—Emotionally Satisfying Flavors

Every BonBon has a binkle center. I like to say: "If you know what a binkle is, you're in the binkle movement. And now you do, and so you are."

Welcome. May your life be a bed of binkles—for yourself and everyone you touch.

Binkles are an essential component of experiencing a BonBon. Its message is not just for the heart, or for the mind, but for all of you. It sparks awareness. It reinforces feelings of enjoyment and good will. Your enjoyment is made all the more pleasant because each morsel is a celebration of your animating energy. (See more in Chapter 1.)

I coined the word "Binkle" in 1992, and my life has never been the same since. All of me – my mind, emotions, and body (both individually and together) – assesses each experience as to whether there are binkles present. When the situation or person is binkle-deprived, I don't linger.

But high-binkle people and events call to each of us, so we can connect in a most delightful way. There's a lift, a resonance as we engage and recharge each other. No words or prior contact are required.

A binkle is a measure of energy, like an ohm or a kilowatt. Except that *you are the meter for sensing its presence and intensity*. Binkles charge and delight every part of you with an influx of buoyant energy, that makes you feel most alive. And *all of you* delights in basking in their warm glow.

And sharing them? That just releases more... and more... and more... Binkles can go viral in the truest sense of the word. Not every BonBon in this chapter is directly about binkles, but all speak to that energy. Help yourself.

- Love Is Lovely
- Every Binkle Is a Moment of Freedom
- Binkles Are Pixie Dust
- Embrace Your Authentic Impulse
- How Binkles Are Different than Just Plain "Happy"
- Putting Civil Back into <u>Civil</u>ization
- Word of the Day—Minor Meanness
- Choose Something Else
- Make a Space for Grace
- Recharge Your Binkles
- In Praise of Our Limitations
- My Heartfelt Wish for You

LOVE IS LOVELY

Dating services and websites have something to teach us. They know the lure of relationships, of affinity, of connectedness is valuable in its own right. They call it "chemistry." Close, but the attraction is really a matter of responding positively to another person's *energy level and intensity*. It is physical—but so much more.

That drive to find "someone special" is much more pressing for every living person than a mating dance. It's a universal desire that's not exclusive to finding only one match or one kind of connection.

Gender, age, marital status, sexual preference, amount of wealth, and educational level don't matter that much by comparison. The urge to find connectedness is written into our DNA, reinforced by brain structure and an array of hormones and unconscious triggers.

It's the emotional hunger we sense long before we can talk. It's the basic need to love and to be loved. Although it has a central place in sexual attraction, it's equally important for other warm relationships. Close family ties, cozy community activities, and innermost friendships are often peppered with love vibes.

Love is not well served by Hollywood or the romance industry, that obsess about the trappings and the wrappings. They're focused on externals—the appearance and deft slight of hand. Those matter little when love is felt, and are a poor substitute when it isn't.

Every single contact with someone else can be an opportunity for an exchange of love. Not the kind that breaks up marriages or invites being molested. Rather, it is an exchange of our essential energy—my "who I am" with "who you are." It's not arising as the outer package, but through our *energetic fingerprint* that each of us displays.

83

Brief or long, one time or many, close friend or a stranger. That spark, which signifies an energetic alignment, leaps beyond having a personal connection. That subtle surge of energetic affinity can be felt in every cell of the individuals involved. But it also creates a ripple that's felt by those nearby, and expands to all humanity. That sensation reminds each of us that love is the universal tonic for "what ails 'ya." Lovely indeed! It's the smile felt in every cell.

It's nice when that energetic resonance shared. But the drive to find a specific or special person can blind us to the many ways that spark is lit in our lives by the people we encounter every day. A person who is in love with life can feel such a rush of buoyant energy at any time, any place, or with almost anyone.

That splendid sensation needn't be rare, for its allure can be glimpsed around every turn. Grasping it brings happiness and joy—a "this is perfect" moment.

Feeling that special energy deserves to be savored—clasped for a moment to appreciate its preciousness. As it happens, you sense being linked together by *something more*, by the etheric, energetic "cobwebs" of love.

When you begin to notice that energy, recognize more of those experiences of yours your life as love, how can you doubt its presence? How could you feel unloved? *Your lovable self* is the very essence of what you hunger for. And it's already yours.

Lovely, isn't it?

NOTE: This one doesn't say Binkles directly, but that's exactly what this BonBon is about. A binkle is the smallest particle of love or positive energy that can be felt between one person and another, and between you and yourself.

Every Binkle* is a Moment of Freedom

*"Freedom is actually a bigger game than power.
Power is about what you can control.
Freedom is about what you can unleash."*
Harriet Rubin

You're totally free when you sense a binkle. It disengages you from deep-rooted influences, personal baggage, long-held habits and limits, and inertia that sucks the oomph out of life. Each is a new beginning—if you choose to treat it as such. Binkles are an injection of energy—the joyful, upbeat kind. It bubbles up and bursts into a sensation of delight.

It is a pivot point. Poised to move forward from an unlimited new space—albeit a tiny one. You can enlarge it—keep it engaged and growing as you pursue and enjoy the binkles that arise in your path. You'll find them when feeling their characteristic zizz.

Claiming your freedom is about wholeness. All of you: mental, emotional and physical. No preferences. The mind and emotions sometimes can escape their physical limits by leaving the flesh behind. Until all of you participates, you're simply flirting with being free, however.

True freedom is beyond "freedom *from...*" or "freedom *to...*" which are both related to things beyond yourself. It puts the emphasis outside, rather than inside. Freedom is a paradox, not relative to anything beyond your essential nature. You recognize your true identity, which knows that it is always free.

Now is the only time and place when you are truly free. We know about Now moments and understand that's when you're most alive and living fully. Isn't it wonderful to know every binkle is a "now"—right Now! But it's not simply being out of the stream of time—neither past nor future.

Each binkle provides re-charge station that instantly renews you. Energized, poised to proceed without limitations—and free. Now, where do you want that sense of liberation to take you?

When you're having binkles you have already won your freedom. You can *feel it*!

Binkle – The energy that's created when two people really connect.

BINKLES* ARE PIXIE DUST

Magic stuff! When sprinkled into any situation, onto any person or crowd, it makes what's happening glow.

Glow with:

- Good will for those on the spot, and for those you hold dear

- Upbeat energy that brings a smile to your lips and a twinkle to your eyes

- Delight and joy—it just feels good

- Good humor—likely to erupt in giggles or roars of laughter

- Bright ideas—brilliant what ifs...

- Lightness of heart—without a care in sight; buoyancy

- Radiant warmth that those you encounter can feel

Binkles are the effervescent energy that come from connecting with an open heart. Open to life. Open to others. Open to being surprised. Step forward with a binkle instead of from your ponderous and weighty mind. Lightheartedness sets a whole different tone to interactions.

You'll find yourself flying... over the customary obstacles, over the fears that stifle the urge to take risks (or fly), over the yucky stuff that consumes too many hours—starving your vision and satisfaction. Binkles take you riding on a buoyant updraft of vitality.

Whatever happens when you're powered by binkles seems very much like magic. But how it works is as solid as gravity and as consistent as a law of physics.

It's Binkle Power!

Binkles are a force of nature that can leap tall problems with a single bound. Or a single chuckle.

Binkles make you fly *and* glow. That's SUPER!

*Binkles—the energy that's created when people really connect.

EMBRACE YOUR AUTHENTIC IMPULSE

Who is the you with vision? Who is the one who sees the world as *it could be*? Who is the one who sees yourself as *you could be*?

That ability (nay, urge) is embedded in each of us, in our deep inner recesses. It is out of the spotlight or the glare of clamoring expectations. It is unique in the form it takes, for each person has his or her own inimitable outlook that holds onto a wistful hope.

That impulse is what gives rise to the wee small voice. That is the authentic impulse to do what you are alive to do. It urges you to be true to yourself and to make a difference. That unique and specific drive is not a theoretical wistfulness, but it sets a very real possibility that you have the power to achieve. It is a tangible part of "who you are"—"who I am."

So, the question is not whether visions of "something more that is possible" arise in us. It does and will continue to do so. The question that needs to be asked by each person is: Why don't I embrace it? What am I doing *instead*? What do I consider more important?

You want more passion in your life? That authentic impulse is the source of passion—the genuine article that makes everything else pale by comparison. It cannot be faked. It cannot be satisfied by trifles.

Anyone who taps into that, even a little bit, feels a momentary desire to move heaven and earth to live up to that transcendent awareness. So why is the wholehearted embrace of our vision so rare?

We know the answer—the why notes:
- It's hard
- Life gets in the way
- Our responsibilities and expectations come first
- People wouldn't approve
- We don't trust it on one grounds or another
- There's no time—of course that's only because it's not a high enough priority

There are really good reasons why to ignore it, deny it, foreswear it. But even so, that won't be the end of it. Something in you wants to emerge and will keep piling up. Give yourself permission to let it guide you. Make a poster you see every day:

Embrace Your Authentic Impulse

Water the sprouts of insight with your attention. Marvel that you "know" something that's amazing. Let it flower for yourself. Acknowledge its signs in others.

That is how the world is remade—with a grander vision at the very root. For it isn't about scale or function that gives the impulse its value. It is about being rooted in authentic awareness. That urge may seem impulsive, but it's your genuine self trying to flex its muscles.

How a Binkle* Is Different than Just Plain "Happy"

Lots of things can make us happy—for a moment.

- We're pleased to get what we want—or something even better
- We really love being liked or appreciated
- We can't wait for things to turn out the way we want them to be
- We live for the days when we know that our life has a meaningful purpose
- And more...

But some ways we make ourselves feel good aren't good for us—or anyone else,

like:

- Using power tricks or manipulation of others to make things go our way
- Undermining those around us in petty or self-dealing ways
- Enjoying addictive habits and practices that let us escape our responsibilities or what we agreed to do
- Blaming the world for our problems and mistakes
- And the list goes on...

So, a person can feel happy without the joy of your heart bubbling up. But then there's a sense of something missing.

Binkles are always accompanied by joy in some form or another

You feel a zizz of energy rippling through you—whether a slight tremor or a full-fledged Wow! Of course, happy and binkles usually appear together. But when you feel negative feeling about somebody (or yourself) there's no place for joy. No binkles. How sad.

Take a closer look at what makes you happy. If there's there no upbeat energy present, no binkle, some sort of deception is going on. Maybe it's a half-truth or fudge about what's happening. Or it could be from a self-deception you've lived with so long you no longer doubt its erroneous message.

It's your job to tell the difference between what you call happy and the joyful energy of a binkle. If they're the same, wonderful! Otherwise, look for the "worm in the apple." To find the offending distortion brings an unacknowledged "lie" to light. It's replaced by a truth that can set you free. You'll know you've found it because of feeling the binkles and a blast of joy.

Remember, there's no such thing as a negative binkle. Your heart can always tell the difference between a real one and a fake, even if your mind gets fooled sometimes. Your body knows as well—by the energetic zizz it feels. (A fake binkle is draining and takes you down a notch.)

Don't settle for less than happy *and* binkles—now that's a happy thought!

*Binkle – The smallest particle of affectionate energy that's created between two people. You can feel it.

It started with a riddle. Someone I greatly respect was given this conundrum by her spiritual teacher many years ago. And she would bring it up for discussion from time to time. Like a Zen koan, it does not have a simple answer. The question is designed to be pondered until the intellect throws up its hands and steps aside. That capitulation could yield an aha! moment.

Why did Jesus go to the lowest?

There are lots of answers, and you can surely add your own:

- Compassion
- To teach by example
- To show charity toward the unfortunate
- To prove he was a good person
- He saw their need and was moved to take action
- They were willing to believe in him
- To save their souls
- It was the loving thing to do

But to me the real and paradoxical reason Jesus went to them was, **he did not see them as any different than himself**. He recognized those less fortunate as one with him—the child of the same God. Instead of noting their differences, he focused on their sameness to him.

Jesus didn't treat people according to their status or economic condition. Their needs and desires were (and are) no different from everyone else's. And they're no less deserving of love and kindness. He acknowledged them sharing a common humanity.

Jesus refused to accept society's view that certain people, or groups, or beliefs, were lesser or flawed for some reason. By going to them, he ignored sanctions against socializing with them. Doubtless, Jesus knew that seeking out social rejects would provoke puzzlement or antagonism about himself. But he didn't explain his motives.

Jesus spoke often about being motivated by love—it's the essence of the Christian message. **Love cherishes what each of us has in common, no matter what form it takes**—and the rest doesn't matter as much. Seeking out those whom others dismissed as not good enough demonstrated his love of them.

Why don't we give it a try? That would put civil back into civilization—certainly it's a step in the right direction.

THE WORD OF THE DAY— MINOR MEANNESS

I saw one the other day, and then because I was in the mood to spot them I saw more. And once I knew what I was looking at, I started to notice they were everywhere. They are so omnipresent that it's not surprising why people tune them out and let them pass.

Acts of meanness, no matter how small, deserve to be pointed out, objected to, called to account, rather than being overlooked and treated like they don't matter. Because they do. Make no mistake, there's covert, underhanded abuse being dished out as casually as passing a plate of cookies. That poisons the way we treat one another.

I wondered why we don't look

- Perhaps it would hurt too much to accept the implications of such treatment

- Perhaps we'd want to return them in kind (and maybe we do)

- Perhaps we'd look petty and quarrelsome, or over-sensitive

- Perhaps it's not "nice to notice," so we silently tolerate being disrespected

- Perhaps we'd feel more defensive and less safe

I'm not talking about major meanness or overt evil here. Those harsh verbal and emotional assaults *are noticed*, objected to, puzzled over, and acted upon to make them stop. And because they are impossible to ignore, we are forced to deal with them somehow. Since they're not delivered in such a sneaky way, major meanness is more likely to be sorted out.

By contrast, minor meanness is largely ignored, allowing it to fester under the surface. There it eats away at us like termites undermining our foundation. But because such disparaging treatment is often repeated, its long-term effects can be very destructive. Many relationships are riddled with so many minor meannesses that there's little else going on between the parties.

The worst part is that much of the minor meanness is delivered by "nice people" who consider their behavior acceptable. They act like those oh-so-trivial lapses of consideration are OK.

But they aren't pleasant things to do or say to anyone. Ever. They're certainly not pleasant for the one who just felt the ouch. So how come "nice people" do them without a twinge of conscience or hesitation?

As long as we're inclined to let minor meanness pass unchallenged, it will continue. But before long it erodes the trust we count on with each other. So, let's name names. Where in our interactions do minor meannesses thrive in disguise? A few that come to mind include:

- Gotchas and told you so's

- Faultfinding—the pick, pick, pick variety

- Demeaning jokes and humor that holds someone up for ridicule

- Insults delivered in the guise of useful information or neutral facts

- Put-downs and sarcasm (notice it's really sour-casm)

- Catty, venomous, or snide remarks

- Withholding a thank you or compliment when it is deserved

Minor meannesses simply pile up until we notice them and say "Enough!" The pressing question should be how to stop them. Imagine—if we don't engage in minor meanness what could we put in its place? How about Minor Kindnesses and Major Kindnesses?

CHOOSE SOMETHING ELSE

Every moment we respond to life. The true choice is not what you do or say. That's secondary in time and significance.

The choice is—Who in you will respond?

- What you always do—your habits and ego, *Or*
- Something else

A binkle* is evidence of "something else" at work. Two things occur at the same time. The first choice *did NOT happen*. So, something new and vital (as in full of life) is about to show itself. And with it comes a zizz of buoyant energy that charges the moment with significance. Even the angels hold their breath in anticipation.

How will the spark of divine energy express itself as "something else?" What unique flavor of yourself will color the next moment?

Your next move could be inspired—a creative opportunity grasped. It might be a tendril of new possibilities springing forth, unconstrained by prior limitations.

What will become of it? Only time will tell. Some tendrils grow and yield a constant supply of similar positive energy. Some fade from memory. But each such wisp of possibilities ruptures the mindless *status quo*. Each leaves its mark on the moment and the people involved.

That's momentous! It's the definition of world changing. All from choosing something else.

Life moves on. The next moment... Another response by you...

It could be habit or "something else." Can you see why that's a big deal?

*__Binkle__ – The energy created when two people connect. Or when you connect with anything that inspires you (even yourself)

MAKE A SPACE FOR GRACE

God comes in the little spaces between—between activities, between thoughts, between people. That's the brief moment where there's a "space for grace." It's not felt as grand and glorious, but close and intimate—because God becomes alive to us that way. That's really how we connect—not through large gestures but in the wee, small, personal and intimate ones.

But for that to occur, we must leave space that's unfilled with other matters. Make space between all those jostling concerns sucking up your attention and energy. Make space for the presence of God, and it will be filled.

Space between events bring peace and freedom
    (though brief).
Space between people brings respect, and often love.

Space within yourself brings joy.

P.S.   Make a space for Binkles!
      Every space IS a Binkle!

RECHARGE YOUR BINKLES*

Binkle – Binkle – Binkle – Binkle…

Did you feel that? It's a little jolt of energy from me to you. It's physical. You can feel it as it recharges your battery. A Binkle is a tiny, yet perceptible charge that occurs when two people really connect. It's the smallest packet of interpersonal energy.

Whether the contact is brief or long, whether or not words are spoken, it's the truest form of communication. Once engaged, it makes other types of communication carry more meaning. A binkle is also the antidote for stress, since each tiny surge replaces the energy drains that deplete you.

Each person you encounter, whether a nameless clerk or to your spouse, could use a Binkle. So could you. You can't give a binkle without receiving one. Pause to connect—look him or her in the eye, crack a smile, say something kind, and sincerely acknowledge them. Almost instantly, there's a momentary connection, which is accompanied by a zap of energy. That's all it takes to be a Binkle Ambassador.

Enjoy the sensation, the other person, the uplifting energy, the moment, which you can prolong indefinitely. Every binkle leaves good will in your wake and adds a bounce in your step.

You can Binkle by yourself (like when you enjoy a sunset) or in a crowd. The important thing is to binkle—whenever you can, however you can, and as often as you can.

Disclosure: There is a binkle in every BonBon

* A **Binkle** is the energy that's created when people really connect.

IN PRAISE OF OUR LIMITATIONS

Learning to appreciate the value of our personal limitations is the beginning of wisdom. A person has to live with disappointment and failure repeatedly, and has been "to hell and back" before realizing:

- Each of us is most unique in our personal limits and warts, for those are the battle scars from being fully engaged with what comes your way. In our accomplishments, we resemble others who managed to do the same thing.

  Achievement gets the praise and attention, rather than the "whatever it costs" doggedness that kept you hanging on. Pity. Resolute endurance beyond what can be borne is much more valuable in developing your character

- You can learn more about your inner identity from what you've disliked about yourself than from what you're most proud of

- Our aspirations lead us to grow and change. But we shouldn't ignore what is already solid at our roots. Our limitations anchor and sustain us as we tentatively step out. They should be pruned to *grow with us*, rather than being considered barriers or something to be discarded

- How you choose to express or suppress your inadequacies creates the fuller-realized you

- Limitations that are faced, but not rejected, provide the transformative power to make us stronger and more discerning—rather than them being thrown overboard as excess baggage

- Our limits keep us humble, which is just about the only thing to hold the self-centered ego in check, allowing us to turn toward the larger reality the ego is blind to

- Our inadequacies spur us toward being ever more creative and enterprising in order to compensate for what is lacking. And they lead us to express an unconventional approach that reflects our unique abilities, coupled with what's been learned through living

- Our limitations make us need others since nobody has all the skills and knowledge (let alone character and moral fiber) that we require in life. We're designed for cooperation and collaboration

Making peace with your limitations provides needed perspective as we strive to make the most of what life hands to us. They make us do more with what we have, than we ever suspected was there. And they often turn out not to be handicaps at all.

NOTE: This in no way resembles resignation. For our limitations provide the impetus to keep growing and changing in ever more remarkable ways.

My Heartfelt Wish for You

Gratitude has welled within my heart for all things good.
With your permission, I'd like to state the obvious.

Best treasure those in your life who have integrity
in their own lives.
There are so few of those. This is a tie.

Best treasure those in your life who have a wise thought.
There are so few of those. This is a tie.

Best treasure those who are dependable.
There are so few of those. This is a tie.

If we can have friends such as these, if possibly have a
friend who is all three, we must hold that one dear. That
person is worth more in your life than all the money,
position, and power there are to be had. Let us be grateful
for those ties that bind us close with them.

More yet, let's each strive to be one of the those who is all
three. That can be your gift to me. And me, that will be my
gift to thee.

PS And here's a load of binkles to brighten your day—
binkle binkle binkle binkle binkle binkle binkle binkle binkle
binkle binkle binkle binkle binkle

CHAPTER 5
NOUGATS—NEW GUTS:
CHANGES AND RENEWAL

What is required before you take the need for making long-resisted life changes seriously? Are your goals the "one of these days" desires that are dreamed about, but pushed aside for later? Do yours arouse a burning desire that gives you no peace unless you're driven forward?

The primary motivators for change are discomfort (anywhere from mild to your pants are on fire) and desire. That, too, can range from a mere preference to such an intense urge that nothing else seems worthwhile.

Either way, for change to actually happen, the desire for it has to move out of the category of good ideas you merely think about to it being *something you actually do*. What becomes a passion must be a priority that shoves competing desires aside. It needs drive and urgency to give it focus, to give it life.

To accomplish something new requires putting your effort into it—making it a commitment. Imagine how much more exhilaration is felt when your desire to make a difference in life involves reaching for the stars—rather than swatting away fleas.

Such fervor makes a greater difference to the world, and the rest of us, too. Come what may, that level of drive is a turn-on.

- Ask Not for Whom the Bus Comes…
- Build a Better Mousetrap *Maker*
- Ligatures of Devotion
- In Praise of My Body
- Exalted State of *Becoming* Unapologetic, The
- Trap the Phantom
- What's Wrong with Abundance?
- Truth Comes in Many Flavors
- Window Washing Time
- Cranking the Starter
- A Winner in Loser's Clothing
- Lessons I've Decided Not to Learn
- Arrive Within

Ask Not for Whom the Bus Comes...

And Jesus walked along the lake until he came upon some men who were fishing. And he said unto them, "Follow me."

And one of the men said unto him, "Would you mind coming back when the fish aren't biting?"

And so, he left.

Opportunities present themselves in many guises. Some are humdrum, as easily caught as waiting for the next bus. There will be many other choices along soon.

Some other opportunities have the possibility to be life changing. If it's not embraced quickly and with the right spirit, it will be gone—never to return for you. If you should miss it, decline it, ignore it, that indicates that it's not much of a priority in your life. It's **the bus not taken**.

Who knows if there will be another one as providentially designed for you. The question to ponder—can you tell the difference?

BUILD A BETTER MOUSETRAP *MAKER*

Ralph Waldo Emerson sounded the rallying cry for innovators: "Build a better mousetrap, and the world will beat a path to your door." To the sorrow of many who developed their own form of a better mousetrap, it usually does not work out that way—certainly not as smoothly as they expected. The world shrugs, and those eager to launch "the next big thing" feel misled.

Emerson's essays encourage us to act on our flickers of genius, and many on the visionary path attest to his motivating influence on them. His abiding gift is urging us to roll up our sleeves and do something about our inspired visions. If Emerson's advice is to serve as more than glib rhetoric, however, there better be a mousetrap produced sooner or later.

At a point in my life when I was launching an invention of my own, I had a friend who was a venture capitalist (though not an investor). He told me that before moneymen like him decide whether to back a new product or project, they are especially concerned about *the quality of the person behind it.*

An invention or untried idea cannot stand on its own without the driving force of a committed and capable champion. Investors are placing their money bet on the person as much as on their idea.

They will not risk their money without considering the advocate's track record: Does the person have the needed skills? Are they capable of working out the nuts and bolts of the endeavor all the way to the payoff? Is this their first mousetrap?

As with first love, an upstart creator cannot imagine the world won't want and embrace what they've accomplished—once the word gets out about how great it is. Has he or she survived the disappointments of that naïve phase (sadder but wiser), then taken an idea through the stages to follow? In sum, how likely is the person to pull off what is required?

But there is a larger view to notice as well, beyond the practical outcome of the undertaking. While the innovator developed and launched what they assumed was the next eagerly awaited "mousetrap," they had also been remaking the mousetrap maker (himself or herself).

The person was becoming more vision-focused than before. What they went through in devoted service to their over-riding mission refined their discernment and proficiency. It also expanded their perceptual lens, so they could bring more kinds of know-how and judgment to bear in any future undertaking.

Less apparent, the person was not simply more capable than before, but became a step removed from their prior frame of reference. They had disengaged from where they started, to some extent, and thereby changed their long-term trajectory.

To paraphrase Emerson, "Build a better *mousetrap maker,* and the world will beat a pathway to your door." The world desires and needs *better mousetrap makers* much more than a larger selection of mousetraps. Anyone who can find original and ingenious solutions to what people want, as well as reinvent who they are in the bargain, is sure to make waves.

LIGATURES OF DEVOTION

Inspiring!... Powerful!... Life changing!... Motivating!... A moving call to action!...

The speech was a knockout. Everyone in the audience was touched, moved, and challenged. To a person, they got the message and vowed to follow the call. They were persuaded, willing to make the necessary and desired changes.

Then... nothing happened. Nothing at all!

While it is important to kindle the vision and muster the resolve, that is the easy part. All of that motivation achieves nothing unless you also cut your ligatures of devotion. They bind you and blind you to achieving heartfelt desires, challenging goals, or a greater vision.

These strands may be small, but there are many of them:

- Habits, those things you do routinely without thinking or attention

- Cold slogans and clichés that have long served you, but which have lost their relevance

- Relationships, along with their related expectations, that have ceased to grow and nurture

- Unexamined assumptions

- Dogmatic and slavish devotion to the past and the familiar

- Ways you regularly waste your time, energy, money, and opportunities

- Causes and commitments that no longer suit you or serve you

- Short-sighted values and priorities

- Passivity, indifference, and inertia

- Self-defeating behaviors that lead to unintended, yet predictable, consequences

- Irresponsible desires and activities

- Early childhood programming that you've never examined or outgrow

Each of these ties can be changed or broken in a moment's effort—once you pay heed to their restrictive pull. But you must first notice their presence, their negative influences. They are your *status quo*. Each of them asserts a powerful drag that keeps everything (and you) just the same.

Their tendrils hold you, tied like a prisoner to your own past and unexamined habits. Whenever you break those ligatures of faded devotion, you are like Gulliver, severing his puny bonds. After you're freed from those many small ties, you can move forward—toward your beckoning goals.

Your devotion to many of the old and cold connections doesn't serve you. Inquire, "Does this link bind me to strengths or to limitations?" Sever those restrictive ligatures. Each snip acts as a liberation! Finally, your resolves and desires can move you forward decisively! At last, whatever has inspired you is within your grasp.

In Praise of My Body

It only took a few days of being really sick to bring me a needed reminder of my body's wondrous abilities. Unless it's out of commission I don't notice all the ways it takes care of me and carries on (carrying me onward), day after day, after day.

- I push myself to work hard long hours, ignoring my body's justified pleas for rest

- I exhaust myself in endless matters without considering which are better left undone—ever

- I make foolish choices that do not serve a healthy lifestyle

- I am self-critical, dissatisfied with being too lumpy and dumpy, or performing at less than my best (even when it doesn't matter)

- I take my well-being for granted and treat the need for renewal as a sign of weakness

- I am impatient with my own limitations, lashing myself to go "Harder, Faster, Longer," never satisfied with what *has* been accomplished

- In the name of goal setting or efficiency, I constantly add new burdens and demands, ignoring all signs of progress

And how does my body treat me, despite that? It wants to succeed, and gives its all, even as I neglect and abuse it. I can count on its persistent efforts, as I push forward every day. It delivers renewed energy and enthusiasm for the tasks at hand—when it's needed most. How loyal, how courageous!

It is time to:

- Sing praises for being healthy, which is hardly noticed except when it's gone

- Thank my steadfast side, that never gets its due

- Gambol in joyful and unproductive activities, like a playful child

- Love the unappreciated "dogs body" that's ignored and abused without mercy

- Seek renewal for my heart and spirit, for my mind, and for my body's sake—learning how to be kind to myself.

THE EXALTED STATE OF
BECOMING UNAPOLOGETIC

This is not the ego-driven, in-your-face version of being unapologetic. It is not the assertive form of telling people not to argue with you. You're right, so there!

Becoming unapologetic as an exalted state entails *moving away from having been apologetic*, of cringing, and backtracking. Of having been shamed or ridiculed. But no more.

It is a culmination of a long, uphill, forlorn road where you haven't been on your own side.

You've been apologizing, appeasing, and shrinking back about some behavior or personality trait of yours for a long time. The specific activity is probably not a big deal in itself (lots of people do it). Like day dreaming, being an eager beaver, or a foodie (whatever).

But it has invited criticism or being "teased" on a regular basis. And it's now a tender spot, where you feel self-consciousness and ashamed. So, you avoid it, try to minimize it, or hope that nobody will bring it up. But it keeps coming up, making you feel even more apologetic for the umpteenth time.

Or you could be the culprit yourself, whereby you treat some mannerism or behavior as a lapse. Those self-inflicted criticisms or put-downs become a steady refrain of not being good enough.

Internal or external, those jabs are belittling. They are not minor, for they steal your vitality and focus. Little by little, they rob you of energy and confidence.

Accept that long-standing point of embarrassment unflinchingly and without apology. Embrace the side of yourself that suffered so deeply from those jabs and taunts. Let the self-acceptance flow, along with the knowledge you're not wrong to feel or act that way.

Turn away from the shame you've felt about whatever it is. Accept that it's OK. You're OK. More than OK! This is a moment of reconciliation—without denial, without justification, and without blame. It has no place for self-righteousness—only self-acceptance and happiness. You're on your own side the healthy and loving way. And it's about time!

Rejoice! When you can embrace, without reservation, what you've been apologizing about, you'll discover how being unapologetic is an exalted state indeed.

See the BonBon, "Clumsy Is Glorious" in which I finally embrace the truth that had been denied so long—I'm clumsy.

TRAP THE PHANTOM

Naming a problem gives it form.

- It may not be the whole problem bothering you.

- It may not be the core problem bothering you.

- It may not be the most important problem bothering you.

But you've caught hold of something. Instead of a phantom, a scary and elusive beast, you've managed to capture *something* in your trap. It's not a mirage, not an over-active imagination. Even if what you've grabbed ahold of is misshapen and unfamiliar, you're one step closer to knowing and besting the very adversary that shivers your liver.

- You took action rather than yielding to the amorphous terror of the unknown.

- You dodged the fears which warned you off and made you reluctant to confront it.

- You've got something to study, dissect, and analyze, so you're not just guessing about what you're up against.

- You shined the brightness of your full attention on the insidious irritations and disquiet that hide in the shadows.

But naming a disturbing concern is only the beginning. Next, disengage from it. Treat it as though it is *a* problem, but not **your** problem. Already it has become far less puzzling, ominous, or shapeless.

Once you know what you're up against and can avoid its emotional tentacles, it loses much of its power of intimidation. The threat that brought you to your knees becomes docile and manageable. Yes, there is still much to do.

But having conquered your reluctance to open that door, and all that goes with it, conquering the diminished hairy beast just requires working out the details.

Shorn of its fearsome aura, the problem ceases to be too gigantic or too monstrous for you to subdue.

What's Wrong with Abundance?

The word, "abundance" has been hijacked by the world of things—by the desire for stuff. It's a buzzword for "give me more, ever more—and that still wouldn't be enough." The ENOUGH button has been disabled.

Motivators and marketers are allies in chanting the mantra of "abundance thinking," with books and workshops on how to get it. And how to fix what's wrong with you if you can't. But it's a con—designed to direct your attention from the true abundance you *already have*. The kind of treasure you can't buy with your credit card.

Because what they offer, and what so many people accept without question, is a false promise. The more you have or can get your hands on, the more you are, the happier you'll be.

Sorry, it doesn't work that way. Acquiring more stuff can't bring lasting or deep happiness. It's merely a childish game. No matter how well you play it, the result isn't satisfying. The next new desire forever presents itself.

Abundance has a sister named Gratitude. When the two get together the heart is full. The urge to acquire more is stilled. That feeling has absolutely nothing to do with how many possessions one has. Who cares? Whatever it is, that's more than enough.

That's what true abundance is—pressed down and overflowing. Expanding beyond limits. That's what your heart seeks—not another "must have" to add to the pile.

See through the diminished promises touted by the "abundance priests." Which is your birthright? And which represents a mess of pottage?

Truth Comes in Many Flavors

The first truth to know about truth is that there are a lot of different kinds. All are true to a degree—but they're not equally genuine, accurate, and reliable.

1. Everyone knows

That's the common wisdom of the world; accurate and inaccurate all mixed up together. That's what we're taught as kids and pick up from those around us. Although we don't question it as it comes in, we spend the rest of our lives discovering what just 'ain't so. Still, it's considered "close enough."

2. What I know from my own experience

While it's true you had the experiences, it's seldom that any of us make the effort to place them in context. Besides, we're dynamic and alive. So, what we know and understand changes with time. The truth as understood by a child is very different from the truth understood by an adolescent, or the parents, or the elders.

All versions of what happened can well be true, as far as they go. But each is limited by perspective and experience. Trusting experience adds up to a whole lot of gray and very little certainty.

3. What I believe—the truth you've bothered to check out and commit to

You've grappled with it, scratched your brain and asked sincere questions. This is your best shot at nailing down the truth, so you're willing to rely on it. It's still a mix of truth and half-truths, dogmas and illusions. But, hey, they're yours. And besides, they will change as you go along.

4. Fudge—what's true because I prefer to think so

Oh no, not lies exactly. But it carries a bit of bias we close our eyes to—pretend we don't see. It would be random distortions, but notice there's always an unacknowledged element of self-dealing. Not much scratching beneath the surface or double-checking to get the facts, either. Quiet assertion or hype—same difference.

5. Scientific truth and reasoning

Now here's where objectively reliable truth can be found— or so we believe. Science attempts to analyze and define what's lawful in the world. But its methods are limited and the scope of topics narrow. There's a lot that science doesn't know or can't find out. We've been oversold what rationality and the scientific method can deliver, so settle for facts that are "statistically significant."

7. Big "T" Truth—the eternal, big-picture truths, like the virtues honor and courage

These aren't garden-variety trifling, subjective, defined-by-the-situation truths. These speak to our higher nature and make us rise to life's possibilities. They can make us stretch. So, we don't take them off the place of honor and dirty them up in everyday concerns.

No—we save them for special, in a safe place, where they get dusty from lack of use. Respected, quoted, revered, but without day-to-day relevance.

Sad to say, there's not a lot of demand for big "T" Truth. Most people are satisfied with what they've got already—whether it came as religious dogma, a profound aha! experience, or wise philosophies.

Those who bring Big "T" Truth (visionaries and prophets) are seldom welcomed and often scorned. Their message is usually an affront to people who are satisfied with their own version of truth. And it's always disruptive—challenging "what everyone knows" and "what I believe."

7. Fresh Truth

Beyond even Big "T" Truth is Fresh Truth. It exists in a different sphere because it creates a bridge between theory and function, between the idea and what arises through effort.

Fresh Truth is discovered and expressed by a person attempting to actually live the larger truths (which aren't in service to their ego). Through their devoted struggle to live in accordance with their over-arching reality, the person stretches beyond the truth they know.

That brings truth alive. Perhaps only for a moment. But that's the majesty of living truth—an authentic force for mankind:

- One individual at a time...
- One opportunity at a time...
- One truth at a time...

And that's how each of us can keep truth relevant, fresh, and vibrant.

Window Washing Time

Masks and mirrors. Half-truths, and wishful thinking. How many distortions get in the way of us living straight-forwardly? Those falsehoods don't go away, even if we've long since forgotten how they got into our thinking. Like the gray film on an unwashed window, the layers of imprecision build year by year—unnoticed, uncleaned.

They are not intrusive—but still they do us harm.

It is not heavy chains that bind our precious inner selves and bar our freedom. It is not coercion by malicious foes that blocks our best efforts. It is the ever-present veil of untruth that hold us in thrall, that keeps us cowed and silent. The grimy film accumulates from the countless, thoughtless, less-than-true, unthinking layers that have built up over time.

The accumulated layers of distortion warp our thinking. They muddle your sense of identity—making it rather fuzzy around the edges. Their cumulative presence shrinks your view and the accurate perception of "who I am."

The real person I truly am lies beneath all that, but it's hidden from view too much of the time. But it can be found, even when I've lost touch with that bright and shiny view of myself.

It's easy to think that bright, shining sense of myself is about youth or a recollection from long ago. We've forgotten that our positive and easily delighted sense of identity is still on the scene, even though it gets pushed into the background much of the time.

Dig down layer by layer, deeper and deeper to reach what lies beneath. That side of yourself shows up once in a while—on sunny days. But mostly, the view we see of our undiminished, vibrant nature is blocked by a gray haze—but one that can't be blamed on the weather.

It's time to wash the windows and to strip away the grime. Scrub and polish. Don't spare the elbow grease. Don't defer to familiarity. That genuine identity of your dear self underneath is as unmarked by life's burdens as a newborn babe.

Its innocent, unbroken, unafraid, eager to engage what living has to offer. That's the person at your core. That you that's been kept in the background is wanting to peek out, waiting to be set free.

The layers can be stripped away with suds and water. Push back the curtains. Determination will be needed to avoid stopping before the windows sparkle.

Noticing the presence of the cruddy layers needs to come first. Then a resolve to **see your reality directly** washes the grime away. It's worth the trouble.

CRANKING THE STARTER

Today I got out of my way. It was a shock to discover what had been standing in my way without me even noticing— me. I had thought there were many problems that needed to be solved first. I had thought I had to get ready, to know more, to track down essential missing pieces. I thought more time and planning were required before I could begin. So instead of starting, I kept busy getting ready to start, then getting ready to be ready to start.

So today I *started.* And only after taking that long-delayed step could I see how much fear has gotten in the way. I honestly had not realized I was afraid. I let being busy become the point of it all. I had been doing the best I could. I really was, but I was also fooling myself.

I was unable to see any of my foot dragging while I was so busy getting ready to begin. But, by the simple act of commencing, I changed things in a fundamental way. I stepped out of the grip of my invisible fears. They have no further power to *stop* me now. They only had the power to keep me from starting.

A Winner in Loser's Clothing

The other day I lunched with a dear friend. As we visited, she told me, "Remember Joe? I finally figured out his problem—why we never could make our relationship work. He was a loser in winner's clothing."

The words rang true. Joe was an attractive package: glib, a blossoming career, educated, with well-connected friends—but not much substance. Self-absorbed and superficial aptly summed him up.

Her words came to mind when I encountered a solid-gold friend who hasn't been treated kindly by life. Yet he carried on with good cheer despite repeated setbacks. He never sacrificed his horde of straight-shooting and unpretentious virtues. I saw him as a "winner in loser's clothing."

It reminds me how easily the inner person and the outer person can offer very different faces to the world. But the inner face is the one that endures. I realized that I, too, have been a "winner in loser's clothing" at times. Painful, yes; frustrating, yes; disheartening, yes—*but also temporary.*

Being a winner on the inside requires an extra measure of character and courage. As material concerns are diminished in importance, the inner qualities become even more valuable—more in evidence. I suspect that character only grows its strongest during the down times (a potent argument for occasional doses of misfortune). Character doesn't come and go at the whim of fortune, but is rooted in virtues that last.

A "winner in loser's clothing" can change their "clothing" and outward appearance as confidence returns, and as resources come to hand. Even if long endured, the pain of deprivation or loss is temporary, and not the true measure of the person's value.

But those experiences prepare us for the not-yet-unrealized goal all along—being a winner in winner's clothing.

LESSONS I'VE DECIDED NOT TO LEARN

To learn the wrong lesson from past disappointments or setbacks could easily make me prejudge whatever is about to happen. And that's not something I'm willing to do. I'd rather be wrong and pay the price for it, than to accept where the indicated conclusions would lead me.

Naïve? Maybe, but also, it is an intentional resolve to trust that the world is not a hostile place, but an encouraging one.

When I'm scraped and bruised, humbled, and discouraged from some stumbling block, I know there's more than one message available to me. So, while I want to understand what happened and improve my strategy for the future, I hold certain conclusions in abeyance.

To accept them would make me cynical, world-weary, and suspicious. That is too high a price to pay in order to be self-protective.

Lessons I refuse to learn—despite any evidence to the contrary:

- Not to trust so readily, or to be so self-exposed and vulnerable

- Not to take risks, or that a person seldom wins against long odds

- Not to expose myself to another person too soon or when there is no apparent advantage

- Not to try yet again, after something doesn't work for the umpteenth time

- Not to expect the best out of people when the chips are down—even if somebody has already let me down before

- If it appears to be too good to be true don't touch it*

Each of those lessons (and countless more of their ilk) would diminish my choices and constrict my openness to life. They would make me timid, rather than bold, giving more credence to the potential down side than the potential up side.

Reaching conclusions like these would make me value the pain and disappointment of the past over what lies ahead—though it's still in the possibility phase. This takes courage, not blindness or wishful thinking.

Learning such lessons would probably make me safer and less likely to be disappointed from time to time. But not *every* time. But the downside of accepting those conclusions would mean sacrificing my philosophy about making a better world. That counts for something. Everything, actually.

NOTE: This approach is not the same as Pollyanna. I notice the warning signs and adjust my strategy, but they don't keep me on the sidelines.

* See BonBon in BonBons I, "Ode to Being Had"

ARRIVE WITHIN

Troubled? Stressed? Discouraged? Puzzled? Overwhelmed?
Totally drained? Rejected?

Here's your remedy, that's sure to bring relief:

- Relax and pause
- Trust in yourself—the side of yourself anchored in stillness
- Resist looking for advice and quick fixes—maintain an empty space
- Turn off your mind and the perpetual chatter
- Sense your spine, then your heart—notice they are not "thinking"
- Hold—open and receptive
- Invite your quiet wisdom to speak
- Forget all demands and obligations of the world for a bit
- Defocus both your eyes and your mind

- Ignore the passage of time
- Pause... just breathe
- Respect your answer, once an insight arrives
- Thank the source of your newfound awareness
- Recharge
- Rejoice!
- Re-engage; proceed with assurance

Repeat as necessary.

CHAPTER 6

POPCORN—INSIGHTS THAT "POP"

Consider the lowly popcorn. It is hard, dry, and indigestible. Yet after it endures the flames, the unquenched heat and friction, it is transformed. From being solid and inert, something tasty bursts gloriously out. In a single moment, what is within the kernel is set free, becoming light, enlarged and free-formed. The result is edible and accessible. It is delicious—something to savor then demands another bite.

Can the puffed corn ever return to the constrained limits of the hard kernel? Of course not. It has changed its state as it attained its fullness.

You, too, expand with every insight that POPs in you. You, too, expand when you rise above the friction of life's difficulties. They're the tangible signs of your own wisdom bursting forth. And with it comes a larger, freer, happier frame of mind.

- Des<u>tiny</u> Is Never Tiny
- Glorify the Small Stuff
- "Do NOT Judge" is a Place, Not a Verb
- What It Means to Seize the Spark
- The Problem D'Solver Laws
- Beware of Potential
- Choosing the Cup
- It's Time to be HUM (rhymes with bloom)
- The Gifts of the Wise
- Bridge Across Forever, The
- Beyond Knowledge
- Reading the Signals Defies Logic

Destiny Is Never Tiny

It's easy to be misled—to feel I'm small and limited, just one among many. To make us look around and wonder, "What makes me think I'm special?"

It's easy to chalk our feelings of special-ness up to the ego—to an inflated sense of self-worth, or to yearnings toward grandeur.

Yet, each of us is grand and glorious in ways the ego can't begin to understand. In ways that it can neither initiate nor influence.

You bear a destiny unique in all the world. Capable of transforming the world in manners that are beyond imagining.

And to sense your destiny, even a little, even for a moment, is immense. That surge of awareness reminds that absolutely every step taken with a sense of one's destiny is both immense and significant. When touching your destiny, you can't be tiny.

Glorify the Small Stuff

It is easy to overlook the very small things that are right in life, that lift your spirits without fail, that make you pause and catch your breath in amazement. They nurture you and make you smile—if only on the inside. They appear like flashes of light that flit in and out of notice—but in tiny ways and quiet ways. Their presence makes your life go more smoothly—what a happy thought!

But we put much more concern and energy into those things that don't work as we like. Focusing on disappointments and let-downs is not an intelligent way to portion out our time and attention. It's better to spend it on the small stuff that gladdens the heart.

The light of attention is powerful. Detach it from the loud and jarring events that embroil you in turmoil. Instead, focus it on the delightful little things that light up your eyes. Glorify them! Treasure them! Give your simple pleasures extra awareness so they occupy a larger and more influential place in how you live.

Recognize them as they happen and feel blessed. Pause to savor the silent strength you draw from being attuned to their presence. Embracing the precious wee experiences fills you with gratitude. That creates a brief pocket of tranquility, which can be stretched o – u – t for as long as you can hold onto it.

Gratitude is a mindset that brings its friends, Grace and Joy with it.

Notice, enjoy, share, treasure—these are verbs, action words. Doing them is your part. But in doing your part, the splendid little things you noticed are enticed to show themselves as being much more significant than they first appeared to be. They come out and dance with you.

By opening yourself to what is small and simple, you discover how much your life is filled with delights that have been too long ignored.

"Do NOT Judge" is a Place, Not a Verb

The admonition "do not judge" has been taken to ridiculous lengths in modern life. Even the most absurd, inappropriate, or self-serving behavior rates a pass by those determined not to criticize. Discernment is jettisoned willy-nilly to avoid the appearance of being judgmental or reluctant to understand.

We're all the poorer for it, since relevant nuances of thought and behavior go determinedly unnoticed.

It sounds noble and open-minded to declare, "I won't judge." The statement implies: I don't think I'm better than you. My behavior isn't any different than yours. It further implies external standards don't apply. All words, deeds, and beliefs are equal—even though they are not.

Refusing to judge has become the unchallenged and worthy (see, that's a "judgment" word) objective. A statement of fact (even if totally true) that sounds the least bit judgmental brings instant rebuke from all directions, "Don't judge!"

Everyone is busily not judging… or noticing… or standing up for any notion that could be construed as "better," or "virtuous," or "good for the world."

The problem is, that's a simplistic example of either-or thinking—judge versus not judge—choosing between opposites. Either one is a verb—*something one does*. To attempt to do both (avoiding either one) sounds less judgmental, but leaves one paralyzed.

The phrase "do not judge" has been totally misunderstood and misapplied. It's not about doing something (or not). It refers to resisting the urge to judge (or not), **so you can be free to try something entirely different**. It refers to *a place within yourself* where judging isn't possible.

Go there. Disengage momentarily from trying to change or fix things. Suspend your preferences. Appreciate what's unfolding, without the need to understand it. Without the need to control it. Ahaaaaaaa… There's nothing needs doing. Peace reigns.

See, it's a place within—an awareness, a place of clarity. And its name is DO NOT JUDGE. Whatever makes you want to criticize or "fix" yourself or anyone else is a reminder to go there.

What It Means to Seize the Spark

The spark is more than in insight—a glimmer of a lightbulb going on. That would be quite enough to gain it a place of honor among our everyday thinking. But its power and influence go way beyond that.

A spark of insight ignites other thoughts. It can act like a firecracker: Pop! Pop! Pop! Maybe launching fireworks that make your best ideas shine bright. But it is too narrow to only consider the quantity and quality of the ideas that arise. Look at the energy being released. It energizes! It ignites whatever thoughts you've held that resemble it.

The mind is involved, surely, but so are the emotions, and your body too. *All of you* is united in the energetic surge of an aha! Savor that sensation, along with the light it brings (in all its forms). For that brings more light (delight) into your thinking, into your life.

Each spark is a call to action. It comes with an imperative: Do something with this! Fan the flame so it grows brighter. Bring it into tangible reality. Let its novelty carry you away. Blow on the flame so it grows brighter, and brighter still.

Sparks of inspiration release energy. And when taken to heart and allowed to be expressed in deeds, they can have power beyond belief.

It helps to keep a lantern at hand that can keep the flame alive. But insights do not want to be confined to a single small, candle-sized flame. It needs to be spread—shared with others and linked up with concepts you're already excited about.

We've heard the expression, Seize the Day, Carpe Diem, as a rational to grasp the opportunity that is at hand. That's good, but that is a whole different scale than seizing a spark. A day is like a year, compared to the instantaneous awareness of a flashing spark. Many can occur in mere minutes. Speed is necessary, a willingness to act without hesitation.

Seize the sparks that arise within you. Nourish them reverently. For it is your own priceless wisdom offering to play a more active role in how you live. Grab it, protect it, and don't let go.

Seize the Spark
Carpe Sparkem (Latin)

THE PROBLEM D'SOLVER LAWS

*Every problem is an invitation to
open your mind and heart*

1. A problem is a terrible thing to waste. Each is tailor-made for you.

2. Problem D'Solving is a process. Finding solutions changes you *and* the problem.

3. How you define the problem determines the kinds of solutions you get.

4. Every problem is a failure to see. Improve your vision and understanding and the solutions appear.

5. Einstein said, "A problem can't be solved at the same level it was created"—the trick is in finding another level from which to view it.

6. Every problem is a demand for change. The answer must be both more simple and complex than the conditions that led to it. (Resolution always involves a paradox.)

7. No problem or solution occurs in isolation. You have more resources at your command than you initially realize. The problem provides the incentive to look for them.

8. The answer can be found *within* the problem.

9. Answers come from knowing less—not knowing more. Disengage from what's already known and hold...

10. No answer works until you *use* it. Part of the answer is the action taken.

11. No answer is final or complete.

12. Go beyond ordinary, familiar, short-term answers to find extraordinary ones.

13. You aren't done until you're glad you had the problem.

NOTE: As a professional speaker in the 1990s, I called myself The Problem D'Solver.

Beware of Potential

"But Dad…, he has so much potential!"
"This business has a lot of potential…"

The word "potential" paints a beautiful unmarred picture.
It suggests unmixed images of success, achievement, and
delightful possibilities, off there on the horizon, just waiting
for you to claim them. And it's all yours—because you have
the foresight to make a commitment now. Just act now,
sign here, pay now, commit. After all, opportunities like that
don't come along every day…

Sure they do.

Potential is nothing but a dream, a possibility. Yet it is
presented and "sold" with an element of inevitability that
misleads all too often. I'm all for promoting the dream,
nurturing the undeveloped talent, and reaching out for the
grand vision. They're vital for a full and vibrant life. They
justify whatever risks and hard work necessary to bring
them to reality.

There is the key phrase, "hard work." Between the conception
and the reality exists a long path filled with diligent effort,
struggle, frustration, and self-doubt—without any certainty
that there will be a rewarding outcome.

Yes, there is an important role for potential, and whatever it promises is, indeed, possible. But an emphasis on the activity's potential often disregards the prolonged efforts or commitment necessary to achieve it. The desired outcome needs to be cultivated even more when the unavoidable difficulties arise.

Reach for that vision—want it so badly you're willing to pay any price necessary to get there. Be prepared to work like crazy. Then walk into the picture with your eyes open to the full significance of your commitment. Choose it, knowing that getting there will cost you every bit that you expect—and more.

As such, you aren't being misled by the glamorous, tantalizing possibilities dangling like a carrot ahead of the donkey.

Then you'll gear up, calling on all your inner and outer resources—knowing every one of them will be required and tested—to the limit. Only when the goal contains enough reality will your buy-in exist as more than a dream.

There is latent potential in every seed. But thank heaven there's a farmer willing to toil from planting through harvest. The seed is important, vital in fact, but it is only the first stage of a long, arduous, and complicated series of stages—whether that leads to growth or transformation.

Seeds, like dreams, need to be nurtured, and cultivated, and pruned before they're ready to yield their potential. But recognize that to reach your dreams you must be the farmer. A seed starts to grow when it is placed in the ground. Just as your dreams start to become reality only after they're grounded and put into practice—by you!

CHOOSING THE CUP

Some years back, I had a particular cup that had been my mother's. There was nothing special about it—except that it was hers, and she's been dead more than twenty years. But when I would drink my morning coffee, I'd use her cup—as I allowed myself to imagine that she and I were having our coffee together.

That "shared" cup of coffee became a sheltering, gratifying, heartening space for me, for as long as the coffee time lasted. I'd recall memories of times long past, images of our home life when I was young, things she said to me or did for me—for all of us. I would conjure up the people and events and events from my life now that I'd want to share with her, for it was more than memory at work.

That wasn't a time for me to read emails, or plan my day, or cart out the trash. It was her time—our time. While so engaged, whatever wants to come next is kept at bay. And I treasured the space I carved out in my too-busy day when I'd value her presence in my life once more.

For our coffee time keeps my mother's love alive for me. I am reminded that I have always known love—and still do. From her at first. But she also taught me how to love—how to pass it around. It's only fitting that thoughts of her bring that warmth to the forefront first thing in the morning.

Somewhere along the way, that cup got lost. But that coffee time we shared is too vital to my emotional equilibrium to stop. I've named another cup the "Florence Cup," and don't let anybody but me use it.

I've also designated some other cups—named for my dead sister, my mother-in-law, and several others dear to me, but no longer with us.

As I select my cup for coffee, first thing each morning, I silently issue an invitation for that particular cup's owner to be alive for me today. The past we shared merges with the present, and my heart brims in our wholehearted conviviality.

Afterward, that favorite person's presence and affection lingers, and it spreads throughout my day. Keeping them alive for me that way makes me feel more alive with everybody.

After such a warm start, I think I am a kinder, friendlier, more engaged person to those who I encounter later.

It's Time to be HUM (rhymes with bloom)

The world is ready for a genderless pronoun. Having spent several weeks on a writing project, I kept tripping over the he/she and his/her combinations used to avoid gender bias. There's no way a sentence can read smoothly when weighed down by such phrases: He/she should complete the form before attaching his/her check. (There's an urge to say "their" check, but that's plural, so not allowed.)

Men and women are entitled to equal recognition, which includes having their own pronouns. I'm all for keeping "he" and "she" and "her" and "his." We need them and they do a good job most of the time. However, **words like "I" and "you" work every time, without any confusion about the person's gender**.

The World Needs Another Pronoun

We need one more pronoun, that applies to all of us, but only for writing purposes. Just as you wouldn't address anyone as "he/she," you also wouldn't use the new pronoun for face-to-face conversation. "You" really can't be improved upon—working equally well for males and females, singles and groups. We need a third-person pronoun that works as well.

So, I pondered… Certainly, I wasn't alone in this desire. What possible word could logically handle the job? Was I being presumptuous even to tinker with the English language? But, in that light, who hasn't?

So why hasn't someone better equipped than I am done something about this difficulty? Maybe, it's only political correctness that has made pronoun equality an issue.

I'm more than willing to let someone else find the solution. Notice that the infamous "someone else" has his/her hands full already—and isn't keeping pace with demands.

The New, Gender-less Pronoun

Then inspiration struck! We already have the word… almost. It just requires a little reworking: *We are all human.*

There are two problems with adapting the word "human."

1. It's too long, and
2. It has "man" in it

There are many who think "man" only applies to what you raise from boys.

No problem. I cut the word down and kept the part without gender: HUM (rhymes with bloom). It still works: *We are all HUM.*

So, let's see how "hum" works in practice. Already, I see the new word solves more than one grammatical problem. It works equally well in the subjective case (Hum forgot the book.) and the objective case (John gave the book to hum.), as a possessive (This is hum's book.) and as a plural (Hums should read more books.). Notice how nicely it uses "s" for plural and "apostrophe s" for possessive—making it much more consistent than those other pronouns.

A Boon for Letter Writers

Another solution comes to mind, which has perplexed anyone writing a business letter. Forget "Dear Sir:" (which is not really equally good for men and women) or "Dear Ms:" (when you know the gender but not the marital status—and why should you care if she's married, anyway?). Use the all-purpose: "Dear Hum:". To conclude the letter you sign off: "Sincerely hum" or "Hum truly."

So, by now you're asking, what's in it for me? Why should I care about another pronoun? Aren't there too many of them already?

If simplicity, consistency, and political correctness aren't enough, notice that it's a multi-purpose word. It tells the world you're willing to try something new. You're "with it," up to the minute, maybe even part of an emerging trend.

Get Aboard the HUM Bandwagon

You can't say "hum" without seeing the *hum*or of it. Humor often arises from the absurd, and, frankly, hum is absurd. Surely, the world needs more humor even more than it needs a genderless pronoun.

Hum is bigger than the person spoken of. It's a word that can remind each of us of our ties to *hum*anity. We all participate in the grand human experience, which includes everyone who is alive, everyone who has ever lived, and everyone who will ever live. That's a potent thing to be reminded of—each time you use "hum."

Then, in the end, when your life is over and it's time for "ashes to ashes, dust to dust," then you get to be your most *hum*us.

It's time to be HUM. Pass it on.

THE GIFTS OF THE WISE

Matthew, the first book of the New Testament of the Bible, describes how the wise men who had come from afar fell down and worshipped Jesus. And they presented unto him gifts.

And the Wise Men brought the Baby Jesus gifts to demonstrate their great reverence for him: gold, frankincense and myrrh.

Such generous wishes of good will are no less precious for each of us today:

- **Goaled** – The steadfast devotion and courage to reach for your highest goals and mission in life. That includes gold, possessions, and money. But it is so much more that is not so tangible

- **Frank and Sense** – The desire to be frank and honest in service to truth, which needs to be lived with a dollop of common sense

- **Mirth** – The urge to laugh and feel the joy of your wondrous life

And those are the gifts that I offer to you as well—to be enjoyed and shared all year long.

THE BRIDGE ACROSS FOREVER

We adore the concept of "unconditional love," the kind desired beyond anything else. It conjures up being valued and accepted for "who I *really* am"—without needing to prove myself or risk being found wanting.

Love like that sees and appreciates the most genuine and precious side of us. Who doesn't want to feel cherished? We yearn for a life where it can be ours. In our heart of hearts, each of us wants to believe it can happen. There's such a craving for it...

But unconditional love is not unique in that we want anything that is unconditional, as rarely and unlikely as it can be found in our very conditional world.

Some ideas and ideals are treasured for their unconditionality:

- Unconditional Beauty
- Unconditional Perfection
- Unconditional Grace
- Unconditional Integrity
- Unconditional Peace, Truth, or Wholeness

They are alike in their luminescence and the way each of them feeds our spirits. They touch that same, not-to-be-mistaken sense of absolute timelessness. Such moments are the same in their absoluteness and their fullness.

When any of them touch us, even in a flicker, we're flooded with deep satisfaction and joy. Boundaries and barriers dissolve.

They share an unnaturalness that is evident in the way they stand out from the familiar world we know so well. They brook no partiality, no less-than or watered-down version because they transcend the humdrum sphere we inhabit most of the time. Even so, there's no rigidity to them, for they flow with the pulse of the natural order of things—which humans cannot control. Yet we sense their resonance to ourselves, as they point to a larger sphere.

An encounter with something unconditional shakes a person's existence because what is real leaps beyond the accustomed scale of the ordinary world. For that moment, we know an unlimited state even more real than what it eclipses.

That it can be glimpsed at all, however briefly, resonates through all the levels of your being—to where you, too, are unconditional.

That handshake between the Limited You and the Unlimited You is the Bridge across Forever.

What you discover from your own experience is more true than anything you can learn from a book (including this one). And that knowledge will become even truer for you if you share the discoveries with other people.

You graduate from intelligence to judgment to wisdom, but there is something beyond wisdom.

The bridge from intelligence to judgment is experience.

The bridge from judgment to wisdom is character.

Yet, wisdom is solitary. Beyond wisdom is generosity of spirit, where wisdom is coupled with the fundamental human need to share and apply what has been learned.

NOTE: This BonBon was also included in the first book of BonBons. But it bears repeating.

The Rubber Hitting the Road Is the Rub

Things seem to be moving faster and faster these days. The increased energetic influence we've all been feeling (without being able to name it exactly) is hard to ignore—or deal with.

It doesn't help much to know that things are going to be changing faster and faster—hitting with even greater intensity. All of it is helping to "knock loose" whatever is stuck in our lives. It still comes as a surprise. Words like, "I never saw it coming," spring from the lips—giving the lie to our confidence that we're ready to accept whatever comes.

Your Body and Emotions Are Speaking Out—Louder than Ever

That's to the good. The problem is, it's hard to read them—to figure out what they're "saying." Even when prepared to accept their input as true and relevant, what comes in isn't likely to make sense rationally. The mind reels from the attempt, as the undeciphered physical or emotional messages get more insistent.

Ouch! Pain! Anxiety! Turmoil! Confusion! Disquiet! You feel something is pushing for attention—but what does it mean? What's the correct response to it? They stir up the litany of self-doubts: Why can't I "get it"? Am I resisting? Denying? Barking up the wrong tree? The ego and mind are trying to comprehend a message they can't relate to.

Dawning awareness comes from decoding subtle signs and energetic signals we customarily ignore. But the body and emotions are attuned to them—there's a fluency to those meanings. However, lately even those messages are being garbled. People are saying, "I can't read the signals anymore."

As the "road signs" and land marks of one's inner landscape are being moved about, the old markers are not helpful. Not accurate. Not to be trusted. Downright misleading. For now, we must STOP (hmm... another road sign) looking to those markers for guidance.

We can't help wanting to nail things down so life makes sense again. Is it enough to know that's not going to be possible for times of transition? The mind won't like it. Whereas, our feelings and the flesh know that already. That side of ourselves ever doubted we know what's needed to be comprehended already. That's the message they're working so hard to deliver.

You Get the Message by Not "Getting it"—Rather Zen

Accept it. Trust the illogical wisdom written in the cells, and be satisfied to sink into the irrationality of it all. Accept life without a grip on things. Not for good—but for a while. The long-desired answer has arrived, but the mind doesn't get to read it.

Integration—which happens only over time—will bring the disparate messages together. The urge for an answer is replaced with the certainty that you already know—even without being sure what that is. You'll recognize that has happened only when what was previously puzzling and troubling becomes crystal clear.

Until then, enjoy your daily dose of irrationality as a sign of progress. That *almost* makes sense.

CHAPTER 7

TRUFFLES—NOT TRIFLES

The biggest challenge each of us faces (again and again) is being able to tell the difference between what is important and what is not. Under the barrage of so many competing sensations, desires, and social demands, it's too easy to be overwhelmed by all that's on our plate.

In order to get along, too much that is trivial and strident sucks up our time and energy. Too much of what is beautiful, tranquil, and meaningful goes unnoticed. Too bad. We need to feel that there is something beyond more-of-the-same. Something splendid, that makes the rest worthwhile.

There's no hope for the incessant demands of everyday existence will stop of their own accord. Or that we can avoid being pecked almost to death by them unless...

Unless you make the effort to decide for yourself *what's important for you*. Stand up for it. Make what you've chosen primary to other concerns you regularly deal with. Then tune out or downgrade the rest.

Re-cut the pie chart of where your energy goes. Give a bigger wedge for your first choice—smaller wedges for those that are down the list. Then stand firm, despite the protests and resistance.

Prefer the consequential and life affirming over the ceaseless, mindless, insignificant demands on your energy and attention. Banish the clichéd and never-to-be-satisfied voices that drown out your own wisdom. I promise, a diet of BonBons makes those choices easier.

BonBons are sweet delicacies, but they are far from trivial. They speak to what is worthy of our devotion and unshakable for the long haul. They're about what is important, in small ways or large. Each of them reminds you that *you can tell the difference*—and you prefer the good stuff.

- Break Your Wanter
- A Day Late...
- The EXTRA Extra Mile
- A World Apart
- Beliefs Create Destiny
- Truth as a Sharp Instrument
- Eat Your Oatmeal
- Stumble Upon Countless Joy-filled Sensations
- Watch Out for DIS
- Some Life Lessons Can Only Be Learned While You're Down
- Trees? Forest? Which Do You See?

BREAK YOUR WANTER

If you ever expect to achieve a less frazzled lifestyle, breaking your "wanter" is a must. Who wouldn't prefer a less complicated life—one not so fast and crazy-making?

Simplify Your Relationship to Your Possessions

- Less stuff that you own (or are responsible for)
- Less time caring for stuff
- Less space taken up with stuff—both mental space and physical space
- Less time required to find, select, and buy stuff
- Less need to clean or repair stuff
- Less judging and comparing of yourself with others regarding their/your stuff
- Less room in your head devoted to organizing or keeping track of stuff
- Fewer conversations about stuff
- Less effort needed to keep that part of your life from taking over
- Less money needed to buy stuff, so you can stop hocking your future for it

What that "Buys" You

- Money doesn't drive the train (your decision process) since you spend less—but spend your energy in more creative, yet satisfying, ways
- Unimportant things fall away, allowing you to appreciate what you have that matter the most to you

- The non-stop more, more, more... clattering of the runaway train dies away—freeing up so much of Your time and energy that everything else in your life you care about gets a boost
- Rather than having less, you find that you have more—more things that nourish your spirit and gladden your heart
- You discover the significance of three words: "enough," "simple," and "plenty" They're about your peace of mind, rather than the quantity (or even quality) of your possessions
- More breathing room

Do you want your headstone to read: "Here lies a consumer"?

If you want to regain a measure of control and find peace of mind–all at the same time–get off that runaway train. Break your "wanter." You'll do just fine without it—and probably be happier too.

A Day Late...

Not long ago I missed a deadline—not by much, but fatally. Yet it made me utter the oft-heard phrase about being "A day late and a dollar short." I reflected on how that had been a refrain of my mother. Then the world shook and a door opened...

For a moment, I'd seen the unseeable. I grasped a piece of my own ancient primordial programming that had been accepted as fact, long before I could think about such notions. I accepted my mother as a role model, and this was one of her "truths."

It defined the way I'd lived, but it operated below conscious awareness. All these years, this out-of-kilter phrase acted as an implicit standard of behavior, without me even having gotten a vote on the matter. It made me very good at functioning on the edge. It kept me resourceful and nimble, but also a little out of step.

Suddenly, it was blindingly obvious why my rational desires and determined efforts have had so little effect, why prosperity never seemed to linger, why my best efforts yielded so little in the way of money and tangible rewards in return.

Try as I might, I was unable to elude being "A day late and a dollar short." I was blindly oblivious to its inhibiting effects until that very moment. So, close, so influential, so invisible because I'd adopted it as a given so early in my life. With discovery came such relief and freedom!

That self-limiting idea is being plucked out, and its influence cancelled. I am no longer blind to its influence, and can finally bring a wider range of choices into consciousness. Now that old, encoded instruction is exposed as invalid, it can be replaced. Those words lost their power to restrict my life, as they did before.

It is something I must be attentive about, for old habits creep back. But it's in my sights. Bounty can finally replace their miser's grasp that's hobbled my choices.

But much more has happened. The mystery of a thousand unwelcome outcomes makes perfect sense. The energy to deal with the unwanted results, so at odds with my stated goals, has been set free. Ahaaa... more freedom, for the tether has been untied.

THE EXTRA EXTRA MILE

What noble impulses impel us to do an unasked kindness? From what deep spring arises the "milk of human kindness?" For whatever reason, we sometimes step forward and shoulder a burden that's not our own—that justly belongs to another. That's a good thing. For such acts knit us together, in ways that enrich and renew us deeply within the quiet harbors of our private natures. Through experiences of nourishing others, we are also nourished.

So off we go, prepared to go the extra mile—and feeling pretty good about it. We know that we're responding to our noble calling. At first, the happily lifted burden seems light. Gradually it seems less so, as it competes for our time and attention. As it interferes with other obligations.

Still, with a sense of responsibility, we soldier on for the extra mile. Not quite so gladly, in fact it's getting a bit hard to remember what it was exactly that made us step forward. Whatever noble impulse that was seems a long way off—and theoretical in the face of its inconvenience. But hey, it's OK— that's what the extra mile means.

So, we carry on, true to the commitment, determined to be the good guy, someone to be counted on, as good as our word. And for a while the renewed resolve works. But somehow it starts chaffing a bit, certainly more that we bargained for.

Somewhere along resentment creeps in, and from then on, the burden (which wasn't even ours to begin with, after all) seems heavy, indeed. Then, instead of a sense of purpose and kindness, the feelings that arise shift to annoyance and the person's lack of appreciation (irrespective of how much thanks has been expressed). Anger waits in the wings. So much for the extra mile! Enough! Who needs it?!

The Set-up for the Next Stage

Here's what needs to be understood right then. The purpose of going the extra mile is mainly to get you here, to the very point where you don't want to do it anymore. **For that is precisely the place where the dynamics change**. The issue is no longer about the other person, what you've committed to do for them, or what anybody else thinks about it.

From now on, the focus has moved inside—to your most private inner recesses. And an entirely new game starts. Going the extra mile was for someone else, and you got to feel good about doing it. Going the next extra mile (the extra extra mile) is entirely optional... And illogical... And unfair... And impossible to justify. There are no strokes and paybacks to be had for going on. If you don't want to do it, there's no blame, since you've already gone that extra mile.

Going the extra extra mile is done for yourself alone. For taking that next step can only arise from character. It unites you with yourself, who you truly are—yet hardly ever get to see close up. It's entirely different than going the first (extra) mile, for this truly unselfish impulse springs from an inner state where you seldom spend much time.

The extra extra mile abolishes the resentment and weariness, for it connects you to renewed, untapped energy. You love ourselves and all the world! For **the extra extra mile brings freedom, and with it joy.**

NOTE: Be alert for chronic "takers," or that you aren't inclined to be a martyr.

The deadline is firm, looming and critical. With confidence and determination, you throw all your time and energy into meeting it. Long hours, sleepless nights, postponed responsibilities are the necessary toll. The closer that day comes, the more focused your efforts. Too bad you're cranky and your body screams "enough!" from every joint and muscle. That's what it takes.

You soldier on, straining to achieve that goal... and you *almost* make it. Oh, the agony! The heartbreak! So close! The goal was within your grasp... almost. Then it slipped away, leaving you weary, disappointed, wondering why you bothered to care so much, and railing against the Fates. Pause a moment before wallowing in the defeat.

"Almost" is a hairsbreadth from "just barely." There is so little actual difference between them, but that difference is monumental.

One effort catches the boat, but **just barely**—the nearly identical effort misses the boat entirely. The difference in outcomes is as huge as the Grand Canyon. But it should not blind you to the truth that if you're capable of "almost," you're capable of "just barely"—and more!

BELIEFS CREATE DESTINY

Beliefs create destiny.

Not really. Not directly. Not inevitably.

But they help you to connect with your destiny—
>   Or to get in the way of reaching it.

They can lead to action—
>   Or stand in the way of taking action.

A belief acted on with conviction is a creative act.
>   An act infused with Vision, and Commitment, and
>   Intent, and your very own Uniqueness.

It exists! It actually happened. It's real.

Starting with an abstract idea, a belief, you added yourself to the equation, to the moving parts…

And Behold!

Your reality is altered. The world is forever changed.

And in that incremental process destiny is revealed *to you*.

And expressed *as you*.

Truth as a Sharp Instrument

Truth cuts through the many-layered veils of delusion that each of us has so carefully woven. Each of those veils was woven for a reason—to protect our tender sensibilities from what we didn't want to see, didn't want to know, or didn't know how to deal with.

And soon we didn't have to. Shrouded in the protective cocoon of our own making, the rejected vision or unpalatable version was lost to us. And we come to believe the doctored version.

Big T Truth sometimes appears in moments of inspiration or disruption that intrude into our cozy cocoons. On such occasions, Truth shines through the distorting layers, compelling us to see what we long-since decided to ignore. What we don't want to give credence to is still there—ready to be acknowledged and accepted. As soon as we are ready...

The task you choose to follow in response to the gash in the cocoon defines the role of Truth in your life.

Will you:

- Weave back the rent fabric like a determined spider—repairing the "damage"?

OR

- Expand the tear in order to unravel the confining webs of untruth—whatever that may bring?

167

EAT YOUR OATMEAL

I didn't know either of my grandmothers well. We lived thousands of miles away, so visits were rare and never achieved familiarity. Alas, there are so few mental snapshots to define those relationships that never built to closeness.

I last saw my mother's mother when I was seven. Breakfast time at her house stands out in a collection of sparse images. She always made oatmeal with burned toast; there was no other choice. I didn't like oatmeal, so breakfast became a war of wills: hers versus mine.

Minor skirmishes led to the day I was given the ultimatum: sit at the table until oatmeal. I sat there all day. The oatmeal went untouched. I only proved that I was as stubborn as she was. Day after day, our unbending attitudes over that cursed oatmeal ousted the closeness that could have existed between us. Sadly, that lapse was never was corrected during her lifetime.

For me, oatmeal became the symbol of whatever I wanted no part of. But some things in life simply cannot be made palatable, and they don't go away. They sit there, waiting for you to deal with them. As a friend used to say, "You don't have to *like* them, you just have to *do* them."

I, of course, have likened such obligations to being forced to eat my oatmeal—and therefore resisted them. I'm embarrassed to admit that my response was immature, to be expected of a five-year-old, but unsuitable once I grew up.

If I had considered the whole thing a worthwhile challenge, it couldn't have become such a roadblock. I'd have figured something out rather than digging in my heels. But it was a *little* thing that was allowed to fester.

Really, oatmeal isn't scary. Its danger to me was by leading to an inflexible and brainless strategy—oatmeal avoidance. Oatmeal avoidance is old programming which has persisted long after it is appropriate. The resulting resistance and avoidance lead to more unsavory difficulties than the simple situations triggering them.

I'm wiser now. I can face such situations without flinching. I no longer resist oatmeal—or other things that affect me that same way. Although it may not seem noble to proclaim victory over a bowl of cereal, it is! I've triumphed over a long-denied demon, and hence am armed against others like it. Now that I've conquered oatmeal, I am prepared to face other demons that have hidden in the shadows, triggering long-outgrown reactions.

So can you. Eat that cursed oatmeal. Deal with that self-defeating, stubbornly maintained resistance.

Today oatmeal, tomorrow whatever.

STUMBLE UPON COUNTLESS
JOY-FILLED SENSATIONS

"Smelling the roses" doesn't require roses—or a garden or a nose. It just takes a pause for a moment of heartfelt attention. A moment of receptiveness, as you watch, or listen, or smell, or taste, or touch, or any combination of them. Enjoy what floods in. Enjoy it and be grateful for the experience.

For what? For the shimmer of something "special," something sensuous you would otherwise have missed. You would've passed it by without a moment of regret— at the time or after.

Enjoyment is the key. Enjoyment = In-Joy-Moment.

As you paused to fully engage, you captured a transcendent sensation. But can you do it again a few minutes from now? An hour from now? All day long? Why not?

So, what if it slips away! The next moment holds something just as fine. The process never gets old. Whatever is revealed is always there, inviting our notice.

Don't rush that delicious state of awareness. Savor it. Sink into those sensations—all of you. Bathe in a moment of renewal. That's spelled re-YOU-al. That you, that side of yourself that's usually pushed aside in the jostling of competing demands, has been fed.

That sense of yourself closest to your heart has been deeply and fully satisfied. Enjoyment indeed.

WATCH OUT FOR DIS

Feeling a little disappointed about how things are going, a little disapproval about the way the kids do their chores, some discontent about the situation at work? Gee, it's been tough, just one thing after another, with no end in sight. You can change them *all at once*. These aren't problems, you see—they're mind-sets. And you already have the power to eliminate them any time you choose—Instantly!

First notice what's going on—these are "DIS" words; they start with d-i-s. There are many of them: *dis*agreement, *dis*aster, *dis*cord, *dis*comfort, *dis*couragement, *dis*ease, *dis*may, *dis*grace, *dis*dain, *dis*pute, and on and on. Using such words signals that you are in the DIS place. It is impossible to see accurately while you're there. You can't even see the bright side or hope because of *dis*belief.

You've heard of "rose-colored glasses," which make the wearer see everything as rosy (in glowing terms, too beautiful). In the DIS place you wear brown-colored glasses. Everything looks down and brown (or muddy if you prefer). Quick! Take them off! They make the world seem awful (offal), which is the opposite of awe-ful, where you're amazed and uplifted by what you see*.

Once you can spot the DIS you need to *dis*connect from it. Whatever you do next is a step out of the *dis*heartening quagmire. Take a walk. Visit a friend (but don't talk about your complaints—or theirs). Enjoy your kids—or anyone else's. Wash your car (do something physically demanding). Go out for a sundae. Change *what* you're doing, *how* you're doing it, and *with whom* you're doing it.

172

Quickly *dis*engage; *dis*tract yourself. It's possible to change your mind as quickly and as painlessly as you change TV channels. You'll like the new view better—honest. If you don't *dis*tance yourself from DIS, you can expect your life to be melancholy—or *dis*mal.

*This is an example of *frivel*—inspired wordplay

Some Life Lessons Can Only Be Learned While You're Down

- To let go—whether of things, or people, or habits, or bad ideas, or dreams that no longer enliven you

- To surrender to other powers beyond your own personal efforts

- To face up to your doubts and fears, and look them in the eye without flinching

- To gratefully accept from others what you had the power to give or do in other circumstances

- To discover your limits and to find a graceful—and liberating—way to accept them without self-criticism

- To test what is so strong, so central, so enduring within yourself that adversity cannot destroy it

- To find out who can truly be trusted or relied upon— and who isn't

- To push yourself hard enough to discover untapped talents you didn't need before

- To re-examine your beliefs and sort out which are trustworthy; toss those that no longer serve you and re-dedicate yourself to practice those that do

- To see beyond your ego's self-centered maneuvers and deceptions; the ego isn't wrong, but there's a lot it cannot see or understand

- To discover what you most passionately believe in

- To be reminded of our common humanity

- To discover that being defeated isn't more than you can bear—even though it feels like it

- To further simplify what you had thought was essential

- To look beneath the surface, both internally and externally, for answers

- To cease the petty and self-defeating behavior that doesn't make any sense at all (given its triviality)

- To trust that there is good to come from *apparently* unfortunate experiences

- To accept life's bitter lessons, which we assume we don't need or have already learned enough (but apparently not)

- To grow into greater humility and the clarity of wisdom (they're a set)

- To feel deep gratitude for what you still have, no matter how much has gone or fallen away

- To be less willing to judge others harshly, or to dismiss their discomfort as inconsequential

- To discover the paradoxical and unpredictable nature of life; and bow to never actually being in control

- To return (temporarily) to the joyful lack of awareness of a child, since what could you possibly do about eliminating this perplexing circumstance?

- To find your own wee voice that is in touch with all Truth

- To discover who your true friends are

- That being up or down, you still have a body that carries on for you—be kind to it

- That nobody really wants to hear all the bad news; zip the lip; stop complaining

- Just because you've been kicked (intentionally or unintentionally), you don't need to kick back

- That you can recognize how much it costs others to hang on or carry on in adversity—and you can lighten their burdens by not adding to it

- That you are more than, and different than, what you do—but you seldom notice because you're so busy doing, and rushing hither and yon

- However much you've suffered, others have it far worse, and they can benefit from what you know, can do, and are willing to offer

- That no matter how miserable you feel, the sun comes up, and life goes on

There are plenty of hard-to-bear lessons listed here. And each of them indicates challenges to be faced and surmounted—often repeatedly. Usually so many challenges would be daunting.

But the awareness that overrides each of them is that I have the ability to judge whether, or not, a trial still has something to teach me. And what I learn in the process will be a blessing. (Such a list of blessings!)

If I can face the difficulty before me with a glad heart it holds little terror for me. So, this BonBon is not about whether I must face difficulties and learn from them. But do I reach the insightful, positive resolution after I've done so? Am I aware of being better off for having gone through the process?

Trees? Forest? Which Do You See?

Saying: You can't see the forest for the trees

In Praise of Trees

The forest comprises the collected trees, plants, and critters who live there. It includes the overall dynamics in play—large and small, personal and impersonal, short term and long. But make no mistake, individual trees are important! Every one of them.

Each tree (individual) had to struggle to take root and stay alive. Each faced long odds of reaching maturity, of sending out seeds to take root elsewhere. Most seeds never germinated. Of those that grew, some had ideal conditions; while others found a toehold in rocky soil.

The tree that stands tall in the forest might be bent or broken by the elements. But still it grew. It left some marks of its being there. It hosted birds and insects; it spread its roots and put forth seeds. Some never got larger than saplings, while others developed towering canopies. Some types were short lived; others perennial. But despite their marked differences, each started from a possibility—a what could be.

The forest shows no lasting sign of the seeds that failed to take root. Yet there are many more of them than those that sprouted or grew tall. The forest benefits from those less fruitful efforts as well, for all of them were woven into the living ecology.

To set out on a journey does not presage arriving at the destination. But it indicates devoted effort to make something tangible happen. Even those seeds that never make trees still enriched the forest by stimulating other growth. As we grow and build a life, it moves us one step closer to become a tall, mature, and sheltering tree.

EVER GROWING, EVER CHANGING

For the forest to remain healthy, there must be new growth, along with a paring of weak and unhealthy wood. A forest is a combination of seeds, seedlings, saplings, mature trees, and dying ones. They reflect all the stages of the growth cycle, each competing for water, sun, and nutrients from the soil.

If there is insufficient sunshine or water, they all suffer. With severe enough conditions, the survivors become stunted and distorted, even while hanging on.

A forest is alive—growing and continually changing. There is constant new growth, side by side with decline and death. Even the strongest oaks must re-seed or recede. The largest and oldest trees are in danger of becoming rigid, unresponsive, and riddled with wormy places.

There are many different kinds of trees—not all elms or oaks or evergreens, which represent the diversity of artists, philosophers, scientists, political leaders, and ordinary folks. It takes all kinds of trees (plus shrubs, molds, and flowers) to create an ecosystem—not just a tree farm. The wide diversity adds an element of uncontrolled growth to the forest.

There is never a single tree (or several) in a forest. Their large numbers define the space. They protect each other, attract smaller plants, insects, birds, small animals, and microbes that live together symbiotically. And when the parts are out of balance, they all suffer.

IT'S NOT FOREST *OR* TREES

The forest represents the big picture and humanity's march toward our own maturity. Every tree's contribution reflects only a small segment of that grand progression. We must honor the interplay of the forest and the trees, of the different scales of participation. Recognize that no single organism can exist without the intermeshed influences of them coexisting.

The more accurate view is simultaneously forest *and* trees, and more, with you (the viewer) being a participant as well.

OR TAKE THE COSMIC VIEW

At some future point of time, you might even look back from a distant vantage point and put a "wiser you" in the picture. That side of yourself is out of the forest and trees, and sees them both.

Over the stretch of your personal life, you've built that vantage point. That perspective brings out your own sense of a deep connection with what is being seen.

The path that has been trod all along seems clear enough in retrospect. But it is the eye that was being trained to notice the markers: trees, forest, and the larger relationships of which they are but parts. Tread lightly—sensing your place in the larger reality.

Chapter 8

Chocolate Chips – Nibbles of Insight

This chapter could be called Cookie Crumbs or Bridge Mix, or Nibbles. They're just a taste, a biteful. By comparison, a BonBon is rather long and complex. But although these are shorter, each of them is made of the same stuff. They capture a binkle energy and insight.

As with popcorn or a potato chip, a single taste is not enough. Just one more...

Almost all of these brief, pithy sentiments are original to me. But some few might have lodged in my brain from who knows where. There is no attempt to claim the insights of others (if any of these could be attributed to somebody else).

But insights and moments of clarity reveal significant universals since many people happen to glimpse the same abiding truths. Grab a handful and nibble away on this helping of high-octane snack food.

God acts in the interfaces that logic cannot see. But still, the signs of that presence can be seen.

Being wildly eclectic is itself a form of mastery.

Brilliance is demonstrated through your ability to ground a fleeting insight in worthwhile and novel ways.

Ground breakers are usually just tolerated by the public. But what intrepid, creative, vision-driven individuals really want are kindred peers—those who are dealing with the same level of issues, the same caliber of concerns that they are.

All growth occurs at the expense of balance. Growing more capable in another way is a method of dealing with being off balance.

True alignment is not static or stable; it is paradoxical.

Having to endure looking without flinching at your own idiotic behavior is an inescapable step toward gaining an accurate picture of yourself. But accepting your foolishness without criticism is a necessary step to self-acceptance and dynamic balance.

If you're looking for unity, start with YOU-nity. You are the common link for everything in your life. Figure out how all sides of yourself can be fully engaged, and you'll have a very big answer.

Diplomacy is what you say and do when you can't, or won't, or shouldn't tell the truth.

It should never be confused with the truth.

The closer you are to speaking the truth, the smaller the audience for it becomes.

You can leap tall obstacles in a single bound of insight.

People who truly walk on water do it quietly. They don't make a splash—or comment about it afterwards.

Meddling is not seen as interference by those who do it. They see it as help, and are likely to take offense when their suggestions are challenged or ignored.

To know yourself requires that you discover your own inconsistencies—those places where you are still not integrated or coherent. What makes them praiseworthy is that you're no longer blind to them.

God doesn't want a flawless person. What God wants is a person whose flaws don't define them, or block their vision or courage.

Paradox is the only container that can "hold" the divine within our reality. Anything else is too static and fixed in time. You need the interplay of two contradictory forces to create a dynamic connection. Even if a resolution of the contradiction comes it will not hold.

Some part of me knows I am more powerful than the forces which oppose me.

Why, oh why is that so easy to forget?

No pain. No catharsis.

Devil's Bargain – The little lie that turns out to come at too high a price—often costing your integrity. Is that a trifle or monumental to you?

Notice that sometimes you're planting seeds for what's coming to you while you think you're stuck in the mud.

They say, "The devil is in the details." So is God.

Humility is an underrated virtue. Humility is also an underrat*ing* virtue.

Each of us is most unique in our individual warts, in our specific limitations. They're what make you special for they have been forged by life. You cannot fully accept yourself until you love your flaws as well as the admirable parts.

Put civil back into *civil*zation.

Make the world a binkler place.

Saying: The natural state of man is joy.
But also: The natural act of man is play.

Give your wee small voice a megaphone.

Sacred cows graze in your comfort zone.

Walk softly and carry a big binkle.

More vision = Less division

Let the cherishing begin!

Build a better *mousetrap maker*, and the world will beat a pathway to your door.

Every problem is an invitation to open your mind and heart.

Seize the spark of inspiration
Latin: Carpe Sparkem

A Toast to You and Your Future

May your days be filled with uplifting energy wherever you go

May your every breath recharge and relax you

May you exude happiness and goodwill for all who cross your path, and

May you never forget that all you desire is here already, or no more than a breath away

Each moment of your day is a gift. Open it—see what all is there. Treat it as though it is special. Any moment that you catch, open, and enjoy will lift you out of the ho-hum frame of mind. What a treat! Don't fret about the ones you don't notice.

Never whine or sigh when faced with a difficult challenge or a lesson to be learned. Accept without complaint, or you won't get the message that would have made all the discomfort worthwhile.

Anything you attempt to do is capable of being a disappointment. But never let a less-than-desirable outcome make you sorry you made the attempt. What you actually did counts as progress because you truly did something. Just keep going and build upon what was discovered (or set free).

Kindly and Kingly
They're really not that different. To see the nobility in another—whatever their circumstances is to recognize the kingly/queenly in yourself.

So you treat them kindly—the perfect response to anyone.

There is nothing to gestate if you're not pregnant—pregnant with an idea, a dream, a burning desire with an urge to be born. No one would be alive today if labor was optional. It is the compelling urgency of creation (physical or symbolic) that provides the life-altering power.

It's the "why" not the "how" that imparts meaning. Unless you care about *why you do something*, the rest is just about *how*—the details.

A civilized society cannot exist without many people being civil I's. Be a proponent of a kind and supportive world. Say "I am a walking example of how I want to be treated. That's the root of civil-I-zation.

Being willing to stick your neck out doesn't mean you can't see the risks. It doesn't even mean you think the risks won't affect you. Or that you'll rise above them somehow.

Instead, your attention is focused on something much more important to you—something that you want so badly that the possible dangers along the way do not have the power to block your efforts to reach it.

Half-assed is better than no ass at all. Effort counts.

The way to get grounded is to acquire what you learn from being ground into the ground (mud).

Your ideals are like a music box. Open it often to let the melody flow out. Then dance to that tune as you go through your day.

There are some things you have to do *before you're ready*—or before you think you're ready. Taking that step *anyway* is the crucial element that makes you ready.

It's not smart to turn your back on your heart.

True love shows up when you treasure another person, warts and all, so much that you wouldn't want to change them. They are perfect in your eyes.

Paradox is a two-fisted gorilla. The only way to escape one fist or the other is to shift your focus to include both of them simultaneously.

Let the cherishing begin! And let it begin with me. And let it ripple out like a rock thrown in a pond. Let it send forth a resounding binkle for everyone it touches. And let them bathe their own lives with the full force of their binkle energy.

I Care... but not today.
What you get instead of what you want from somebody who claims to be helping you

I Care... but not about you.
The treatment you get from somebody who doesn't respects who you are.

Stoke your life with binkles and they will keep you warm and happy.

The Divine never gets tired of finding new ways to be engaged in life. Each of us is designed to serve as another original and unique way for that to happen.

Imagine yourself being endorsed by somebody or a being that thinks you're great. It can even be imaginary. What would you choose for yourself?
It's all in good fun.

Cat approved human
Dog approved human
Horse approved human
Parrot approved human
Fairy approved human
Unicorn approved human
Elf approved human
Alien approved human
Dragon approved human
Dinosaur approved human

The spirit of Improbably Events walks the land

Aspire Higher

Seize the Spark

You CAN tell a crappy book from its crappy cover

Be the Kind Kind

The Muses hang out at my house
Fairies hang out at my house
Angels hang out at my heart

What feeds your heart?

BONBONS IN ALPHABETICAL ORDER
Chapter is in parentheses

Popcorn - Insights that "Pop" – Chapter 6   133

Soft Centers – Emotional Flavors – Chapter 4   81

Truffles – Not Trifles – Chapter 7   159

What Makes a BonBon? – Chapter 1   13

Made in the USA
Middletown, DE
08 July 2017